MARKETING MATTERS

SELL MORE BOOKS

WENDY H. JONES

Wendy H. Jones

SCOTT AND LAWSON

CONTENTS

Published by Scott and Lawson

www.wendyhjones.com

Cover Design by Cathy Helms of Avalon Graphics LLC

ISBN: 978-1-913372-01-9

To all those authors who have helped and supported me throughout my writing and marketing journey. Your support has meant so much more than you will ever know.

To Lisa McGrath for all her help and support and for taking the time to proof read this with little notice. I am eternally grateful.

ACKNOWLEDGMENTS

To all those who bought my first marketing book and said it changed their view on how to market and promote their books. Thank you for the encouragement and all the very best with your writing and your continuing marketing endeavours.

INTRODUCTION

I have been marketing my books since I wrote the first word of *Killer's Countdown*, my debut novel. Now, seventeen books down the road, the way books are marketed and sold has changed in many ways. I wrote my first marketing book, *Power Packed Book Marketing* three years ago and as the marketing landscape has shifted so dramatically, I felt it was time for a new and improved book which incorporates new and improved, tried and tested marketing methods. Please note, this contains many of the elements of the original book and whilst some chapters have been re-written they are from *Power Packed Book Marketing*. They do, however, look at things from today's marketing perspective rather than that of four years ago. There are also several new chapters, reflecting more recent changes in the way in which we market our books. One thing you can always guarantee in life is that everything changes. Keeping up with those changes is crucial if we are to ensure our marketing endeavours are successful.

Therefore, I felt there were enough changes and new material that warranted this being a marketing book in its own right, rather than merely an updated original. I am confident that all authors will find this book useful even if they purchased my previous marketing book.

1

MARKETING AN INTRODUCTION

Why Should You Buy this Book?

THAT IS A VERY GOOD QUESTION. I think I can safely say, if you've picked it up, things aren't going so well with your book sales and your finances may be tighter than you would like. I'm hoping you are not quite at the penury stage yet. Or you may be right at the start of your writing journey and you've been told you need a marketing plan. Your reaction may have been, "What! I've not done anything yet." So, why should you shell out good money for this book? Let me, if I may, provide you with the reasons why this is a purchase you cannot do without.

IN TODAY'S rapidly changing world, many authors feel when attempting to market their books they are shouting into a void without as much as an echo in response. Countless authors report not only that their book sales have fallen but, in many cases, flatlined. If that is you, this book will help you to address this and give you greater confidence in your abilities.

WHETHER YOU ARE A FIRST-TIME AUTHOR, new to marketing your book or an author who feels your sales are going nowhere, I am confident this is the book for you. No matter into which camp you fall, congratulations, you have taken the first step towards making the changes required to turn your flagging sales around. How, I hear you ask? The answer - you have picked up this book up from the shelf, demonstrating your commitment to yourself as an author as well as your commitment to your author business. You are, in effect, demonstrating your commitment to getting *your* books into the hands of readers. You are considering the purchase of, or may already have purchased, a book designed to get you off to a flying start or give you a considerable boost up to the next level of sales. Either way, you have nothing to lose and everything to gain. What's the worst that can happen? You sell more books. What's the most exciting outcome? You sell a lot more books. You're a winner either way.

IN ADDITION, believing in yourself and your abilities is crucial to the marketing process. In fact, I would say it was central to everything you do. If *you* do not believe in yourself and your books, then why should potential readers believe in you? This book will help you to cultivate that belief, as your confidence in your abilities grows whilst you work your way through the chapters.

. . .

INSIDE ITS CHAPTERS you will find simple, and yet extremely powerful, tried and tested strategies to help you with marketing your own books. Each of these has helped me in more ways than you will ever know. You can use them as they stand or use them as a springboard to develop your own marketing ideas. Some of the chapters will contain exercises. Whilst you do not have to do these exercises, I strongly advise you to do so. Yes, I know, you feel like I'm ordering you around but there's a good reason for this, not one of them being I am a retired army Major. Honest gov. The reasons are all to do with you becoming a better marketer. The exercises will assist you in moving your marketing plan forward, will allow you to recognise the steps you are taking, and recognise just how far you have travelled. Track your sales alongside these exercises, allowing you to measure the return on your investment (ROI). In many instances this will be an investment of your time rather than your money. Still, time is a precious commodity these days and it is worth evaluating if you are using it wisely. It will also allow you to assess which of the techniques work best for you and help you to focus more carefully on those areas.

BY THE END of the book you will have a robust marketing strategy which will support you in revolutionising your book sales. What are you waiting for? It's time to step out, confident in your abilities to -

Sell More Books

HOW TO USE THIS BOOK

You can read it through from cover to cover and get cracking, dip in and out of it, or choose the chapters that interest you the most. Whichever way, it will provide you with help, assistance and ideas in the areas where you think you may be struggling. If you are already marketing your books there will be chapters that will more usefully meet your current needs. Feel free to start with those. However, reading all the chapters may give you fresh insight and ideas – that eureka moment which could just turn things around for you or be the impetus you need. In whichever way you approach it, I would like to reiterate, I strongly suggest you use the exercises. They are there to get your creative juices flowing. Creative? "I'm selling books, not writing them," I hear you say. But yes, marketing involves some level of creativity. As you complete the exercises let your creative brain take over and turn your promotions wild. I currently have a blue buffalo, which is wearing a kilt, as part of my marketing arsenal. "But Wendy, you write crime books," some of you may be shouting. You're right, I do. Doesn't every crime writer need a kilted water buffalo? More on that later.

I would like you to think of the craziest ideas you can come up with in each section, and then decide which of these you will put into practice. Heck put them all into practice. The sky's the limit. In fact, no it's not, the farthest galaxy is the limit. Be sensational. Putting every idea into practice will also let you know what works and what doesn't. You never know, it might be that wild idea that finally pays off. Not only will you find your book sales go soaring, you'll also have fun. Yes, that's right, you'll find marketing and promotion can be fun.

What's that you say? No, I'm not joking. Marketing can be lots of fun and I am testament to that. I have fun every single, enjoyable, marketing day.

WHAT IS MARKETING?

In its basic sense, marketing is getting your book seen by the people who like, want and/or need it. Also, readers who do not yet know they want, like or need it. In other words, it is letting readers know your book is available. Simple. However, it is, in effect, so much more than that. It is using as many different techniques as possible to get your book seen by as many readers as possible. You need to be aware of who your customer is and what his or her needs are. In order to sell books, you need to get inside the head of that customer and market your product in a way which will reach out to them.

Please note, the last sentence said, reach out to *them*, not reach out to you. It is human nature to think the only methods which will work, are those to which you personally respond. There will be marketing methods you love. There will be marketing methods which you loathe and detest when others try to market their products to you. I can guarantee these are most often the methods you shy away from. Time and time again I have authors say to me, that won't work. What they mean is, it wouldn't work to entice me - personally. However, the bottom line is, you are not trying to sell the book to yourself but to others.

That bears repeating – you are not trying to sell the book to yourself but others.

If this is something you struggle with, print it out and pin it above your desk. In huge letters. This is key to your entire marketing strategy.

I want to go back to something I mentioned earlier and am wondering if you took it in. I said your book is a product. Many authors, especially when they are starting out, describe their book as their baby. Whilst that provides a nice fuzzy feeling, your book is seriously not a baby. I will say it again, it is a product. A product you love, one about which you are passionate, but a product none the less. And like any product you need marketing prowess and a marketing strategy to help it sell.

I digressed slightly there (or perhaps I didn't as this is a key consideration), so going back to our original discussion. Each reader will respond to completely different approaches. As Joanna Penn states in her excellent book *Successful Self-Publishing: How to Self-Publish and Market Your Book*, marketing is about tapping into the emotional reaction of your readers. You need to appeal to the emotions of your readers in any way you can. This is what will sell books. You may hate Instagram, Twitter, Facebook or Pinterest, thinking others feel the same. Wrong. There are millions, in fact billions, of active users on these platforms. Here's a breakdown as of January 2020

Global Social Media Users 3.8 Billion
    Facebook 2.45 Billion
    YouTube 2 Billion
    Instagram 1 Billion
    TikTok 800 Million
    Twitter 340 Million
    Pinterest 322 Million
    (Source smartinsights.com accessed 4th May 2020)

When my original marketing book came out in March 2016, TikTok did not even exist. Yet, it has now overtaken both Twitter and Pinterest in market share for users. I will be discussing TikTok in greater detail later in the book but if you are wondering what it is – a Chinese video sharing network. Video is becoming increasingly more important in the marketing sphere and this is something it is imperative to bear in mind. There is an argument that attention spans are going down due to the rise of digital media platforms; therefore, a 30-second video can capture attention and say as much as something which is written in several hundred words.

These figures are for active users, those who are engaged in, and with, the platforms and using them regularly. That's a lot of people. Take a moment to consider how those numbers would soar if the figures included occasional users who might just catch your post. That's mind-blowing amounts of users.

Many of them will be readers. Why would you deliberately choose to ignore a huge swathe of the population when it comes to marketing your books? Why indeed? I will be covering social media in greater detail later in the book.

This is only one example of a marketing method where you might feel uncomfortable using it in this way. There may be others you come across. Please think of this in a positive rather than a negative light. These platforms are your chance to think of new and innovative strategies to make them work for you in a way in which you feel happy.

One caveat here, please don't make yourself miserable. When I said marketing can be fun, I meant it. I am asking you to try new things, to take a step of faith, and move out of your comfort zone. Sometimes it might be a massive leap out of your comfort zone; however, you may just surprise yourself. If, after giving it a good go, you find it really isn't for you, then it is probably time to re-evaluate.

WHAT MARKETING IS NOT

Marketing is not spamming the heck out of everyone and everything. This counts in both the real and the online world. You are a person not a writer. Just as others are people, not police officers, plumbers, lawyers or teachers. Yes, being a writer is a part of who you are but not the whole. You need to connect with individuals not just shout, "Buy my book," from the rooftops. If people are interested, then genuinely talk about your book, if not, talk about something they are interested in such as talking about the books they like and their favourite authors. Genuinely engage in conversation. Leave your books aside. They may be interested one day or they may not. Treat people as individuals not potential readers or customers. Marketing is definitely not annoying people but engaging in a natural way. To coin a current phrase 'Be nice and treat others as you would like to be treated'.

WHY MARKET?

I would like you to consider a statistic for a minute. I heard recently that 42,000 books per week are now being published. That is up from the data from a Nielsen seminar I attended 5 years ago, which was then 26,000. I am not saying this to make you despondent and give up. However, it is increasingly important that your book stand out from the crowd. It is not going to sell if no one knows about it.

It is generally accepted in marketing circles that for a customer to buy a product they have to have seen it, or heard about it, six or seven times. This means they have to have seen your book cover six or seven times. Your blurb; six or seven times. The look inside; six or seven times. Comments about your books; six or seven times. I'm sure you get the picture. Readers may be reticent in shelling out good money for a new author. The more they see a book cover and blurb, the more likely their brain is to take in what they are seeing. Once the brain starts seeing a product everywhere, it is often a natural progression to think, 'this must be good'. You will get the occasional drive-by, but on the whole, it is familiarity that sells new authors and their books. I get people saying to me, "Wendy, you are everywhere." They are right, I am. Because my marketing strategy embraces a whole smorgasbord of opportunities I have taken to get my books in front of readers. In a non-shouty way of course. Non-shouty is key here – remember buy my book seldom works.

Think about this question for a few minutes:

Are you an author, businessman/woman, or both?

I am hoping the answer to this question is both. However, writers are often shy and retiring by nature and many don't like the marketing aspect of the writing process. This may be how you feel. However, to misquote a phrase, this is not the time to hide your book *under a bushel*. If bushels are your thing, then under one is exactly where your book will stay. No one can buy a product they have never heard of. I am sure the fact that you have bought a copy of this book means that you are serious about getting rid of that bushel once and for all.

Exercise

1. Buy a notebook you will use for your marketing ideas. Carry it around with you and every time you think of an idea, write it down.
2. Write down what you are already doing. I can guarantee you, it will be more than you think.
3. Identify what has been effective. Analyse why it has been effective. What was it you did that led to sales? This is key.

You want to spend more time and money on effective marketing approaches.

4. What did you feel was less effective? Analyse why. What could you do differently in future? Another key point as pouring time and effort into ineffective marketing approaches is counterproductive.

4. Write a pros and cons list of marketing. This will clarify where the blocks might be that are stopping you marketing effectively.

5. Brainstorm as many marketing ideas as you can think of. Add to these as you work your way through this book.

If you have not yet done anything to market your book, then there is no need to panic. The best time to start marketing your book is right now, whatever stage of the game you are at. Do so by starting your marketing plan. You cannot do anything about the past, but you can do a lot to change the future and that future is exceedingly bright indeed.

If you are about to start writing your first book then the good news is, the time to start marketing your book is right now. Yes. That's right, the minute you write the first word. Tell people that you are writing a book and generally what it is about. This means the genre, not the whole plot from A to Z including your hero's inside leg measurement. As the book progresses give updates. This will build a buzz and readers will be ready for the book to launch. Building a buzz is another key area in building success. Please note, I said *building* success. It's a process rather than an end goal. Success requires ongoing work and commitment.

Whilst you are reading this book, I would like you to be thinking about the ways you can implement these strategies into your own life starting today. You should be thinking about how these could fit into your own marketing arsenal. If they do not exactly meet what *you* feel are your requirements, think about how you can adapt them to your needs.

Visualisation Exercise

Sit somewhere comfortable and close your eyes. Picture yourself looking at your royalty statement or your KDP Dashboard (more about this later). Your book sales for one of your books have gone through the roof. How do you feel? How would this change your life at the moment?

Do this exercise five times per day.

Now, what do you have to do to make this picture a reality? Think about that. Write it down.

Now, what would you sacrifice to make this picture a reality? Think about that. Write it down.

It's now time for action. Identifying what you can give up is only the first step. *Plan* to give it up and take the relevant steps to do so. If this is watch less telly, then get rid of that subscription. Not only will you have more time for writing, you will have more money to put towards marketing. This is a double whammy. However, make it realistic and achievable.

What I have written on the next page is important. So important I've left it for the big reveal.

Once you have done this write down in large colourful letters.

I am an author who deserves success.

Pin this above your desk and refer to it regularly.

Believe you are an author who deserves success. Why? Because it is true.

It's time to change your mindset and your attitude towards marketing.

2

TYPES OF MARKETING

Chris Syme has written an excellent book called *Smart Social Media for Authors* which is now available as an audiobook. In it she identifies three types of marketing:

1. Paid.
2. Owned.
3. Earned.

WITHIN THIS, there are a veritable plethora of strategies which can be used to help market and promote your books. This chapter will give an overview of each and outline some of the different tactics which will be covered in these pages. There may be some crossover between these but, in many cases, that is the nature of marketing. There will be some blurring of the boundaries, but that will serve to emphasise the importance of the different ways in which they can be used.

. . .

IF YOU ARE GOING to market effectively, using all available channels, then you will need a marketing budget. In the previous version of this book, I said that this doesn't have to be the size of the GDP of a large country, or even a small one, but you will need a budget. However, in today's book marketing landscape, your budget will need to be larger than I suggested just four years ago. It is a fact of life that 'Pay to Play' is becoming increasingly more important. I appreciate that many writers have little money to spare, so initially you may want to focus on the methods which are free or extremely low cost. However, it is worth saving money towards the cost of paid marketing. Think of what you can give up and use for this. Regardless of the amount you save, it shows commitment to your marketing plan, and more importantly, to you as an author and to your writing as a business. I must emphasise this is your business and I would encourage you to answer this question, "What other business would run without a marketing budget?" This is an investment in you and in your future as an author.

PAID MARKETING INCLUDES - PAID ADVERTISING, fliers, posters, postcards, banners, and renting stalls at book and local fairs and events.

THE CLUE IS in the name for this next one: owned marketing is advertising that you personally own and can control. The largest investment in this category will be your website. There are many sites which offer free website builders and you may want to start off with one of those. However, if you want your own domain name, then a paid website is the best, and indeed the only way to go. I will discuss this later

in the book in the chapter on websites. Other owned advertising are social media accounts, blogs, newsletter, email list,
podcast, postcards, posters, etc.. As you can see there is
some crossover between owned and paid. One large caveat
here. Other than your website, mailing list, and newsletter,
you do not truly own any of these. If you are on any social
media site, you cannot fail to have seen the major changes
which occur on a regular basis. These changes throttle your
reach and encourage you to use paid advertising to reach
your audience. Keeping up with the changes to Facebook
and other social media sites is almost a full-time job in itself.
However, do not be despondent, there are ways to keep up
with and implement the changes in a manner which will
benefit you as I will discuss later in the book.

EARNED marketing sits under the banner of social sharing.
This type of advertising includes: guest blogging, interviews
or guest spots on podcasts, interviews on radio shows, book
recommendations from readers or bookshops, book reviews
and sharing on social media. Never underestimate the
power of this form of marketing. In many ways it can be the
most powerful tool you can use. It is also the one where you
have the least control over what happens.

I HAVE a policy of always saying yes and then worrying
about the aesthetics later. Whilst that may not be something
which would suit you, I would encourage you to consider
taking advantage of any opportunity which comes your way.
You may feel uncomfortable at the thought of speaking on
the radio but it is a lot less daunting than you think. Trust
me, I know. I said yes to appearing as a guest on a radio

show and this led to me presenting my own show on books and writing. You never know where opportunities will take you. Whist I am no longer doing this show for various reasons, I did it for three years and I am now doing a podcast. Once you have said yes, your brain will start to think of ways in which you can meet that obligation. Even if you're panicking at the thought of what you have agreed to, your unconscious brain will be working its creative magic in the background. In order to stop the panic, do five things:

1. Sit somewhere quiet and take ten deep breaths, slowly in and out.
2. Imagine the completion of whatever you have agreed to do. Imagine how you will feel and what this will do to improve your book sales. Imprint that in your brain.
3. Brainstorm ideas as to how you will reach this.
4. Formulate a plan of action.
5. Put the first step into action.

THERE YOU GO, that wasn't so difficult, was it?

WHEN IT COMES to social sharing it is crucial you remember one thing: the more you share and help other people, the more likely they are to do this for you. It is no use expecting others to help you if you do not help them. Be generous, share, like, comment and post about other authors' news and new releases and when the time comes, you will find this happens for you. The clue is in the word social – this is not a solitary pursuit but a collaboration between friends and supporters. The overall result is then greater than the sum of every individual part, to steal and mangle a phrase.

EACH OF THESE – paid, owned, and earned marketing – individually - will help sell your book. However, taken together they can form the basis of an extremely powerful marketing plan and help you to sell many more books. So, take time to explore each and analyse how they can help you. I can hear you say, *time*, I've precious little of it as it is. Now you're advising me to spend more of it away from writing. It's a fact, no matter how unwelcome, that time is currency when it comes to marketing. In fact, it may be the biggest currency you will invest. Marketing is a crucial part of your business, meaning you should be prepared to invest time in its success. This is a chance to turn things on its head. You are banking time which will result in sales, thus paying for that time.

IT IS important to remember that no one strategy alone will reach everyone. Different readers respond to different types of marketing so it is important to ensure you use as many approaches as you can. However, as I said previously, it is not worth making yourself miserable in the process. If using a certain type of social media or attending book signings is your worst idea of hell, you may want to consider these carefully. Only you can make a decision about which route you want to go down and to what lengths you are willing to go, in order to reach the reading public. Whichever way you look at it, one thing is clear – books do not sell themselves – readers need to find out about them.

. . .

<u>EXERCISE</u>

1. Take each type of marketing in turn and jot down where you are currently.
2. What are your strengths and weaknesses in each?
3. Draw three columns in your notebook headed - paid, owned, and earned.
4. As you go through this book, jot down in the relevant column what you could do to make your marketing stronger.

3

KEEP IT PROFESSIONAL

The first, and most important, part of your marketing strategy is to make sure that your book is professionally written, designed, and produced. If you are traditionally published, then you may have little control over this. One would hope that publishers will ensure this happens, and fortunately, this is usually the case. However, if you are an independent author, you do have responsibility for quality control of all aspects of your finished product. Make sure you approach it as a professional. There should be no difference between a traditionally or independently published book.

THE SAYING, *you can't judge a book by its cover*, may be true, however, readers *will* judge your book by its cover. It is, literally, the first thing they see in a bookshop or online. If a cover doesn't suit, a prospective reader goes no further. Trust me, I'm a reader and if the cover looks shoddy, home-made, or does not suit the genre, I move on. I have bought books just because the cover drew me in, and I knew I wanted to read it. Often, these are in genres which I do not usually read. So, the cover is a lot more important than you think.

You should take the time to look at examples of book covers in your genre. What sort of covers do the best-selling books have? What is their design like? It is worth spending some time exploring this. I am not saying copy the covers exactly but make sure the elements suit the genre and the time period. Your books may be historical fiction but the cover needs to appeal to a modern reader. If you look at the classics, many of them have been reprinted with a more contemporary vibe to the cover. Traditional publishers often reissue the books with new covers which meet the current market. What appeals to readers changes every few years. I am currently changing the titles of my books, so the text is larger which is the current trend. You need to be flexible and willing to adapt to ensure sales continue to rise.

Another important factor when it comes to cover design, is how they look on virtual shelves. Thumbnails are increasingly more important as readers choose books on Amazon, Kobo, Nook and Apple Books. Remember, if someone is looking to buy a book on a kindle, or any other ereader, as opposed to a tablet, they may be choosing your book from a black and white thumbnail. Will it stand out? Is it clear? Does it entice and attract? These are questions you should be asking yourself.

MY COVER DESIGNER, Cathy Helms of Avalon Graphics, is outstanding at her craft. I have people coming up to me at book signings and saying they were attracted by the book covers and it made them want to know more. Most buy a book, and many buy more than one book in the series. A good cover is marketing gold dust. I, personally, could not have done this, which is why a cover designer merits every single penny you pay them. It is worth employing a professional. In fact, I would go so far as to say it is essential. Unless you are a professional cover designer, turning your hand to writing novels, this is not the time to go it alone. Covers which have been produced by self-published authors on a budget, stand out like a sore thumb, if you will pardon the cliché.

THE SAME APPLIES to editing and your author photograph. Yes, this will cost you money. However, you should bear one thing in mind. You are not just an author writing books, you are also running a business. I know I have said this before, but the repetition is intentional. It is worth investing in your business and this is the first and most crucial investment. People are spending their money taking a punt on your book. They expect to have a professional product in return.

I ALSO INVESTED in a professional photo shoot in order to ensure my author photo was as good as it could be. While this may seem wildly extravagant, the results meant it was worth every penny. If I apply to speak at conferences etc. My photo is part of my pitch and lets organisers know I am highly professional and know how to paint my business in a good light. A good professional photo means you take your business seriously. If you have a traditional publisher they may pay for the photoshoot, but in today's cash strapped times it is highly likely this will be down to you. This photo will be an important part of either the back cover or the inside of your book.

. . .

As WELL AS having a professional approach to your book, you also need to come across as professional in whatever you do. This applies equally when you are at book signings, on social media, and even when someone gives your book a bad review. Reviews are for readers, not authors, and you should **never** respond to reviews good or bad. If someone didn't like your book that is their prerogative. Pointing out they are wrong means you come across as a jerk. Of course, if they have been rude or abusive about you personally, then report it through the appropriate channels. Still do not respond. The same applies on social media. Everything you say or do should, whilst being a part of your personality, come across as pleasant and giving the impression you are someone who can be trusted. Picking fights can come back to haunt you in more ways than one. This applies to all your interactions on social media not just the ones about your books. The nature of social media means you are on show twenty-four hours a day, seven days a week, fifty-two weeks per year.

ACTING PROFESSIONALLY, also includes being supportive of others be they readers or authors. You are, by far and away, the most important part of your Book Marketing Strategy. How you come across to others, both potential readers and other writers, is crucial. This can make the difference between readers buying your books or moving on to a different author. It can make the difference between other authors supporting you or ignoring you. Be pleasant, polite and approachable in everything you do, be this online or in the physical world. In other words, be the author you would most like to meet. Support other authors. Celebrate their successes, cheer them on and help them whenever you can.

Support publishers, editors, cover designers and all industry professionals. Everyone is there to do a job and that job is to ensure that readers have the best books possible to read. No one is your enemy or your rival. Often, we can feel like that. However, shove those feelings to one side. We can all work together to ensure books end up in the hands of the very readers who will love them. Different readers like different books, something which is a fact of life. I write crime books and mainly read them. However, I will tell my followers about other genres when friends bring out new books. Just because my readers like crime, doesn't mean they don't like other genres. Or they may be looking for ideas for a book as a gift for someone else who reads romance or fantasy.

I CANNOT STRESS HIGHLY ENOUGH how important this is. Social media can be our best friend as authors; however, it can also be our worst enemy. Saying something online that we regret five minutes later, can have devastating effects. Yes, it can be deleted but by then it may possibly have been shared, copied and gone viral. Don't say on social media what you wouldn't say to someone's face. Trust me, I know how it feels to want to respond and put other people right. We've all been there, at times. Be respectful, be polite and regard other people's views. Whilst it is okay to debate and discuss, it is never okay to be rude or disrespectful in the process. That will lose you readers more quickly than you will ever imagine. The same applies when responding to emails from readers and other publishing professionals. I am sure no one reading this would behave inappropriately but at times our nerves may be on edge. It is better to step back and come back later when we can act rationally.

. . .

WORKING TOGETHER with other authors is often key so, respecting them and their views is extremely important. So is supporting them. I work with many authors in both real life and online promotions. Asking what readers like to read and sending them to the correct author and books is not hurting your sales. If they do not read your genre, ask what they do read and recommend another author they may like. I have been at book signings where an author only writes in one genre. When the reader says they don't like crime/romance/sci-fi/fantasy/horror (insert your own genre here) the author replies, "You'll like this one." You know what, they probably won't. Even if your book contains all of the above, there won't be enough of what they enjoy reading to satisfy their taste. Be helpful and recommend another author in that genre. When it comes to buying gifts for their friends, they will remember how helpful you were and may buy your book as a gift. I've had people ask me how much romance there is in my crime books. I've had to be honest and say not much. If they are looking for a Mills and Boon or a Danielle Steel, my book will not meet their needs in the slightest. Whilst they contain some romance, they are essentially crime books. Sometimes they buy one anyway, as Great Uncle Archie loves crime. I've had people say they read fantasy, we've chatted about the great fantasy writers (top tip: Always know a few top author names in every genre), and they've left with signed copies of all six books in my DI Shona McKenzie Mysteries for someone's Christmas present.

AT THE SAME TIME, you need to be passionate. This of course means being passionate about your books, but also means being passionate about your abilities. If you doubt either of these it will come across to potential purchasers i.e. readers and they will not buy. If you do not believe in your product then why should anyone else? When talking about your books make your voice cheerful and confident. If you don't think you can do this, practice in front of the mirror until you can do it. Your brain will believe anything you tell it to believe and the words coming out of your mouth will reflect this.

Exercise

1. I am sure you are a consummate professional and treat everyone with respect and dignity. However, it's always worth all of us looking inwards and seeing if there are any areas in which we could be even more so. Look through your social media and see where you are on the scale.

1. Look at ways you can improve your score. Unless you are a ten, in which case I salute you.
2. Look for opportunities to help and support other authors or to reach out to readers.

4

BRANDING

Branding is the process of creating a unique name and image, both for yourself and your product. Once you start to publish, it is what will attract and keep loyal readers. You want readers to think about you as the author and your books when they see a certain image. Now I am not advocating you have something like the Nike logo, although you may want to have a logo as part of your branding. There are ways in which you can create your own brand without paying out for costly add-ons. Talking of cost, your cover designer will be able to design a logo, or you can commission one cheaply from fiverr.com. My instinct is always to go with your cover designer as they know you and your brand intimately.

The first part of your brand is your author name. Everything you do should be associated with that name. This may be your real name, or a pseudonym. My name is Wendy Jones, which is fairly common, so would not stand out on social media or in bookshops - physical or virtual. Also, because there was already an author called Wendy Jones, this had great potential for confusion. This is especially important given we write in different genres. Therefore, I use my middle initial H, making - Wendy H. Jones. Your online presence should also be associated with your author name. Some authors will use the title of their first book or series as their website name. This is not a good idea on a number of fronts, the main one being, hopefully, this will not be your only book or series. What happens when you are trying to promote book six with a website named after book one? I appreciate you have to run your business the way you want to and that is your prerogative; however, my advice would be to use your author name to avoid any confusion. Thus, my website is:

Wendy H. Jones Author with the web address being https://wendyhjones.com

This ties in with every social media site where I am Wendy H. Jones, so it is easy for readers to remember and find me . The easier you make it for readers to find you, the better it will be and the more likely they are to buy books. You want your name to stick in their minds and repetition will aid this. My one exception was my Facebook profile which was set up long before I became an author. Therefore, the H was missing. I ultimately changed this as readers were tagging me to say they loved my book or were reading my book and it wasn't my author name. This led to a lot of confusion, so now I am Wendy H. Jones everywhere.

Branding also includes the genre in which you choose to write. If you write in two genres, you may want to think about having two names. If you are a romance writer and decide to write horror, your readers are going to be a trifle perplexed when they see the genres mixed up. However, I would like to add to this. Since I wrote the first version of this book, I have started to write Young Adult mysteries and children's picture books. When I discussed using a separate name with my publishers, they were adamant I used the same name as for my adult books. The reasoning behind this was that I already had an established platform and readers would buy the books. This left me in a quandary when it came to branding - how on earth do you brand books in three disparate areas? Then I came up with a tagline.

'Entertaining readers from the cradle to the grave'

This makes people laugh at book signings and it takes their mind off the fact I have crime books and a children's picture book on the same signing table. It also means they invest in all the books as they can be used as gifts for all age groups. It is always worth thinking outside the box when it comes to branding and working out the common factor for all your books. Besides your name, that is.

Part of writing in a genre is that people will know what to expect when they read your book. Therefore, you need to find your voice as a writer in that genre. Your writing style and voice is a large part of your branding. Take time to explore this to establish yourself with a unique voice that is instantly recognisable as you. When I started writing humorous crime, in addition to my original police procedurals, readers said they could still recognise the books as mine. I had established a unique voice and that carried over into the new series. This common factor meant that existing readers were happy to invest in reading the new series, something which can sometimes be difficult. However, it also meant I could tap into new readers who may, or may not, invest in my established series. If they do, that is fabulous. If they don't, I am still picking up new readers who like my voice in the new series

Cover design should also demonstrate your brand. Your covers should stand up to the quality of your genre but should also stand out from the rest. My covers all have a scene from Dundee at the bottom of the cover. The top is a scene from the book. Each book has the same overall theme but different images and colour. Therefore, they have a general brand but are distinctive in their own right. My cover designer, Cathy Helms of Avalon Graphics, has done an amazing job, and I could highly recommend her if you need a cover designed or redesigned. Another designer I would highly recommend is Jessica Bell Author/ Musician/Cover Designer. As you can see, Jessica is a multi-talented lady. Both of these cover designers produce high quality work and liaise closely with authors to ensure the final results meet their needs. I will be talking about the Alliance of Independent Authors later, but if you are a member of this organisation, you can also find vetted designers who will often give you a discount on your book covers.

The main characters of your books are also part of your brand. Readers develop a relationship with a character and are genuinely devastated if that character disappears. Some authors have had to bring characters back, with Sir Arthur Conan Doyle and Sherlock Holmes being the most famous example of this. Despite Holmes having died in one book, he reappeared in the next. An explanation had to be given for why he was still in the land of the living, and Sir Arthur Conan Doyle did it with panache. You might be fed up of the characters but you can bet your granny on the fact that your readers will still love them. You need to write characters who will evoke an emotional response in readers whether it is to love or hate them. I read a series of crime books where the main detective barely had a redeeming feature, and yet I read the books because she was so compelling. I also wanted to see if she would develop throughout the series or was too damaged to be a functioning human being in a world with certain expectations. It was the latter. But she was so brilliantly written, I was hooked from the first book to the last.

The way in which you set out your table for book signings is also part of your overall brand. Use props that reflect your genre even down to the table covering. I have a purple tablecloth which shows my books off well. I use props which support crime books such as a dagger and spent bullet casings. I also have the animals from my Bertie the Buffalo books as soft toys – Alpaca, Water Buffalo, Bear and the aforementioned Bertie the Buffalo soft toy. As my books are Scottish, one of my friends made a kilt for him as he was born in a farm in Fife – in real life. The cheeky wee chap really is a Scottish Water Buffalo.

The way you conduct yourself on social media is also a large part of your brand. Yes, we are back to social media and readers expectations. I cannot emphasise this enough. You are your brand wherever you might be.

One way to keep your brand in people's minds is to use part of it in any talks you give or workshops you deliver. The titles of my DI Shona McKenzie Mysteries all start with the word Killer's. Therefore, I have used the following titles for my talks:

- Killer Marketing Techniques
- Writing a Killer Book
- Writing a Killer First Line

- Killer Crime Writing

I have set up groups on various social media sites called *Killer Marketing Techniques for Writers.* You are welcome to join the group and get hints, tips and ideas for marketing your books.

This keeps my titles in the minds of all participants. Remember, writers are also readers. Talking of titles, they should also be used as part of your branding. My series and books are as follows:

DI Shona McKenzie Mysteries
Killer's Countdown
Killer's Craft
Killer's Cross
Killer's Cut
Killer's Crew
Killer's Crypt
Killer's Curse

Cass Claymore Investigates
Antiques and Alibis
Blood and Bones

THE NEXT ONE will be *Cluster of Corpses.* You can see the theme developing here - the alphabet. This branding ties in with similar series in the genre which will allow the reader to identify the type of book immediately.

Branding such as this is about psychology. It is about split second recognition so the reader knows what they are getting immediately and will pick the book up. They do this without recognising, or even noticing, the thought processes which led them to this action. It means they are more amenable to your book and think it is something they would enjoy before they've even read the blurb. I cannot stress the importance of using lookalike branding too much or too often. Subtle indicators, such as these, can help your readership grow.

Fergus and Flora Mysteries
The Dagger's Curse
The Haunted Broch
The Warriors Revenge

Bertie the Buffalo
Bertie the Buffalo Picture Book
Bertie the Buffalo Soft Toy
Bertie the Buffalo Colouring Book
Bertie Goes to the Worldwide Games

Non-Fiction
Motivation Matters
Marketing Matters

IF YOU ALREADY HAVE TITLES THAT do not appear to match, then think of a series title that will tie them together. Best-selling author, A. B. Gibson, had the following titles for his books:

The Dead of Winter

Tracked to Kill
High Voltage.

As they are all set near Harper's Ferry, the heart of the Appalachian Trail. He has branded his books as *The Appalachian Trail Murder Mysteries.*

Yes. It can be a simple as that.

He is also now writing romance books. How on earth do you tie those together I hear you say? Here's the clincher.

'From heart-stopping mysteries to heart-pounding romance'

I believe that is a genius marketing line.

You always need to think of ways in which you can engage readers and keep them in the forefront of your mind. Remember my method of drawing my series together.

'Entertaining readers from the cradle to the grave'

Not only does that make people laugh but it acts as part of my overall brand. Readers will remember it and when it comes to buying gifts, will think of my products.

One final note about branding, the most important part of your brand should be around you as an author, not an individual book or, indeed, series. Series will come to an end but if the reader is invested in you, the author, they will go on to read any further stories you write.

With regards to branding as an author, think on this little snippet. I can tell you all my favourite authors but could not tell you any of the titles of their books. I just know I love the books. Put your hand up if that describes you. The same applies to publishers. I could not tell you who published their books. I am invested in the author. Not the trappings around them. As the word killer is in the title of my books, readers may remember that, but they would seldom remember the second word in the title.

I know authors who have completely redesigned the covers and titles of their books. They did this because they either felt the branding was wrong or they wanted a fresh and modern look. I am not saying you should do this; I am saying it may be something which is worth considering in order to make your brand more appealing or stronger. It is exactly what I have done with this series of books. I thought the previous cover image no longer announced a contemporary and vibrant book. Therefore, I made the decision that, alongside the updating and rewriting, I would change the cover and the series title. The cover sits alongside my *Motivation Matters* Book and together they make up the *Writing Matters Series*. I worked closely with my cover designer to come up with a design which can be carried across a series, fit in with existing titles and look eye-catching on the shelf. I believe this makes it stronger and more suited to a contemporary audience. Yes, it cost me money but in the long run it is a sensible investment as I grow my business. One which I am willing to make and also willing to give up other things to achieve.

In order to sell books, it is vital to elicit a strong emotion within any potential reader. This is exactly what branding is about and what *your* unique branding should do.

Exercise

1. Spend 10 minutes jotting down what it is you wish to portray in your branding.

2. Think about this over the next week. Give ideas time to take root.

3. If you already have books out consider what the strengths are in your current branding.

4. Is there anything that could be improved?

5. If you have books in different genres, think about what links them and develop a tagline that will highlight that common factor.

5

START SIMPLE

Writers often have many objections to marketing. I can almost guarantee you are shouting at least a couple of them at the page right now.

You MAY SAY you are an introvert and that is why you write. You want to spend all day in your office and, like the cat, only appear for food.

Why should you bother with something as vulgar as marketing? It doesn't feel quite right or polite.

You may feel that you hate people marketing to you and don't want to foist it on anyone else.

That's what publishers are for. (Sorry, this is probably not going to happen)

REMEMBER what I said earlier about books and bushels. I hope you are, by now, convinced that marketing is not only necessary but essential. If you haven't got to this point yet, either I'm not doing my job properly or you are slow burner.

By the end of the book I would hope you are as excited as I am about all the opportunities there are to present your books to readers.

OFTEN WRITERS FEEL that they do not have what it takes to market their books that they are not pushy and get embarrassed pedalling their wares. If you feel like this, then I understand. You are absolutely right. You may not have the skills required for marketing. Yet! However, what you do have is - *you*. You are a unique individual with your own distinctive skills and talents. Use these to develop *your* marketing plan. Use them and mix them in with the techniques in this book, to develop your own powerful strategies. Spend some time working out the combination which will work for you. Please note, I did not say this gives you carte blanche to do nothing. You should be marketing like a ninja, using your own blend that will satisfy you and yet bring you more readers. I cannot stress this highly enough. Marketing is no longer an option but a necessity. I know I have said this several times already but it bears repeating. It should be something burned on the forefront of your brain.

CONSIDER THIS. If you believe you cannot market, it may be time for you to change your beliefs. Radical? You bet. But you owe it to yourself. Many authors start with the belief that their nature will not allow them to market, therefore they will not succeed. If this is you, then it is time to turn that belief system completely on its head. Start by setting yourself a goal. This may be the number of books you would like to sell in a month or the amount of money you would like to earn in a month. It may be a goal for the year. Keep that goal in a prominent place. The cupboard above my computer is a good spot for me. It is front and foremost every time I sit at my desk. It keeps me focussed on what I need to do to meet that goal. Then work out what you can do to help yourself reach that goal. It may be mini-steps at first, but you will take bigger steps as you see the progress you are making towards that goal.

Do the exercise below.

Goals

Write your goals in the space below. Use them as a pledge and refer to them regularly.

Goal:

MINI-STEPS TO ACHIEVE this goal

DATE by which you would like to achieve it.

Regular review dates.

1.

2.

3.

4.

Dating your goal achieves two things.

1. Gives you a finite time allowing you greater focus.

2. Lets you analyse where you are and what changes you need to make to achieve it by your desired date.

PUT these dates in your diary. Then enter review dates so you can keep a track of what stage you are at in your journey towards your goal. Once you have made the analysis, review what you need to do or change in order to ensure the final goal date is met. You may find that you are on track or even ahead of time. That's good. You can relax in the knowledge that you are on track and that your efforts are effective. As well as putting them in your diary, also set reminders on your phone. Use all the technology you can to ensure that you stay on track.

YOUR FIRST STEP

In order to identify your unique talents, I would encourage you to do a SWOT analysis. I am sure most authors reading this know what it is, but for anyone who hasn't yet come across it, SWOT stands for

Strengths
Weaknesses
Opportunities
Threats

STRENGTHS

WHAT ARE YOU GOOD AT? Where do your particular talents lie? An example of this could be that you are a graphic designer. Use this talent to develop knock out book covers. If your strongest talent is writing, then apply to guest post on other people's blogs. If you are good at using Twitter, then use it to help others and to get the word out about your books. Many people tend to downplay their abilities. This is not the time to do that. Think of your strengths in every area of life and how these can be utilised to market your books.

WEAKNESSES

WHAT ARE the areas that you feel need to be developed? Identifying these will help you to move them forward. Once you have an idea of where your weaknesses lie, you can develop a plan of action to improve in these areas. Be honest, don't overplay or underplay in this area. Many authors are extremely critical of themselves when it comes to the writing process. This is the time to be honest but not the time to be down on yourself.

OPPORTUNITIES

WHAT OPPORTUNITIES HAVE you got to market your book? These could include speaking engagements, attending local craft fairs, book signings in stores or even newspaper or television interviews. More on those later. Think carefully about this part of the SWOT analysis. Opportunities are greater than you think.

· · ·

THREATS

WHAT IS GOING to get in your way? This could be lack of time to write or to market, not having a budget or anything else you think could stop your marketing endeavours.

THIS MAY BE SIMPLE, but it is powerful. Think about it carefully and answer honestly. It is especially important to be honest with yourself when it comes to strengths. Once you have done so, then use the strengths and opportunities to develop the weaknesses and negate the effects of the threats.

TIME! We all appear to have so little of it these days, with a zillion demands seemingly sucking precious time away. As a writer, you may feel that you can barely snatch enough time to write, much less market your books. This is a fair point. I don't know your individual circumstances or what is placing demands on your time. I do know, however, that it is worth carving out a little bit of the valuable stuff each day, to put towards marketing. There may be a myriad of brief moments where you can use time differently. Here are some examples off the top of my head

1. Sitting in the car waiting for the children to come out of school. Send out a tweet, put a photo on Facebook, or Instagram, or share a pin on Pinterest. These are all things which can be done in seconds on your mobile phone.
2. Wake up fifteen minutes early and look up a list

of local craft fairs. Find one which fits in with
your schedule and book a table.

3. If you are out buying groceries, pop into the
supermarket café. Put your feet up, figuratively of
course, cafés tend to take a dim view of anyone
putting tables and feet in the same combination,
have a cup of tea, and write your blog. This can
be done on your phone, no need to be in front of
a computer these days.

4. If you're out for a walk, take a photo of something
interesting and post it to social media.

5. Order some postcards of your books.

6. Use your train commute time to jot down ideas
for marketing. If you commute by car, use your
phone. Can I add here, I'm not advising you to
drive and write. Anything you jot down in the car
should be preceded by the words, "Hey, Siri," or
"Ok, Google," then any note you want it to take. I
don't want to be responsible for accidents.

7. Do some book research on your mobile phone.

8. Listen to a podcast on marketing when you are
exercising at the gym or out running.

9. Meet with other authors and brainstorm
marketing ideas.

HOWEVER, it may mean deciding in what way you would like
to use your time. How about giving up watching one of your
favourite TV shows and use that time for marketing. It is
about choices, and the choice to spend time on marketing
and becoming a successful author, is yours. I appreciate I
don't have children or anyone else in the house making

demands on my time, so it may be slightly easier for me. I get that. I still have to decide how to use my time to best advantage. You need to make decisions as to what you can do to help yourself free up time. If it means putting the kids in front of the telly for fifteen minutes, so be it. If it means foregoing your Martha Stewart lifestyle, the cleaning will still be there when you return and no one will die from a speck of dust.

I ISSUE YOU A CHALLENGE. Most smartphones will now give you a breakdown of your average time on your device. Take a look and you will be stunned at how many hours you spend on your phone each day. I did this myself and was truly shocked. I was spending at least 3-4 hours per day online. Even taking into account that some of this was for marketing, and I run the social media accounts for two other organisations, this is still far too much time on devices. Pledge to put down your electronics and use that time for writing and marketing. You will be amazed how much more time you free up which can be put towards your business. Use your time online much more effectively and reduce the time suck element to a minimum. You'll be grateful you did and amazed at how much more you get done.

PLEASE DO NOT THINK I am advocating all your free time be used for business. That will just drive you to a breakdown. You do need to have some rest and relaxation as well but look at how you allocate your time during your business day and see what can be done.

. . .

1. Write a SWOT analysis in your notebook.
2. Work out where you could carve out at least ten minutes a day to devote to marketing. Put these in your diary and stick to them. Make this protected time for you and your book.
3. Plan in a marketing retreat. We are all familiar with writing retreats but not many of us carve out such a big chunk of time dedicated to marketing.
4. Work out how much time you are spending on devices and how you can cut this down in order to carve out time for your writing and marketing.

6

BOOK LAUNCHES

Book launches can be physical or online. I will take these separately as each should be approached differently.

PHYSICAL BOOK LAUNCH

Having a book launch in a physical bookshop starts with relationships. This means building up a relationship with the manager and assistants. Buy books, chat to them about what you are reading, and build up a familiarity. They are therefore more likely to be open to your request. The four main bookshop chains in the United Kingdom are Waterstones, Blackwells, WH Smith and Foyles. Since my previous marketing book came out, Foyles has been bought by Waterstones but is still trading with the name Foyles. I have found Waterstones branches in Scotland to be extremely receptive to both book signings and launches. In fact, I have launched every one of my books in the Waterstones store in Dundee, where I live and where my books are set. There are also numerous independent bookshops most of whom are open to events in-store. If you are not in the UK, then approach your nearest bookshop or research the main chains in your area.

WHEN YOU APPROACH the manager of your chosen shop, it is important not only to *be* confident, but also to *appear* confident when you talk. This is where being passionate comes in. This passion will come across to the manager and they are more likely to grant your request. Take a copy of the book and outline where it fits in with the books already on their shelves. This is important. They need to know where to put it in the store. If you say, "It's a sort of crossover fantasy/romance," you will lose them." They have no fantasy romance section in the store. If it is set locally, let them know that. Give them a date when you would like to hold the launch. It is important to be flexible as to the date. If you are planning on providing snacks or food, let them know that. Often, they will agree then and there. They may wish to get back to you. If they don't get back within a couple of weeks, it is acceptable to ring them. However, do not hassle them. You are building a long-term relationship with the bookshop, so it is important to stay professional.

AT THE TIME OF WRITING, WH Smith are actively seeking authors to do book signings. They advise approaching your local store and speaking to the manager. I know a number of authors both traditionally and independently published who have carried out highly successful book signings instore. It is worth exploring all the shops around your area and requesting a book signing.

. . .

THE BOOKSHOP WILL WANT an idea of numbers – not only numbers attending but numbers who are likely to buy your books. They are only going to stock your book and hold a launch if they feel it will be financially viable for them to do so. It is down to you to invite people and make the launch go with a bang. For my first book launch, I invited everyone I could think of. I also placed fliers in cafes near the bookshop and in all the local libraries. As we have fifteen libraries in Dundee, that is a lot of venues where potential readers can see your book. Bear in mind I said that the more a reader sees information about your book or even the book itself, the more likely they are to buy in to the idea of purchasing it. I created a real buzz about it on social media and made it into an exciting event. On the night, it was packed, with standing room only. There was a professional photographer there who did a sterling job of grasping the buzz and capturing it in stunning photographs. We will come back to those photos when discussing social media.

PLANNING YOUR LAUNCH IS IMPORTANT, but you then need to deliver on the night. Tell the audience about yourself, and your writing journey, and read from the book. The questions and answers can be lively, so you need to be prepared for any questions or comments. Make your talk interesting and fun, unless you've written a book on bereavement, then you might want to rethink that strategy. Yes, even talking about writing crime books can be made into a lot of fun.

ONCE YOU HAVE DONE one book launch it, is important to change things up a bit for the next one, whilst achieving the same level of buzz. This may sound like an impossible task, but I can assure you it's not. You need to utilise every part of your already extremely creative imagination and display a willingness to step outside of the box. Examples of the way things can be switched up are:

1. I talked about *The History of Hanging in Scotland* at one of my launches. I write contemporary books, but who doesn't love a good hanging? Of course, I write crime books. If you write romance, this may not be the best approach to take. This is your opportunity to think sideways, upwards, downwards, diagonally and every which way you can, to come up with your own unique ideas. My first thought for romance writers is the history of Valentine's Day. However, as St. Valentine was a Martyr who was tortured and beheaded, you may want to omit that part of the history. But talking about the way Cupid is portrayed throughout history might be a good subject.

2. Another talk I give is about the strange laws you hear around the world. Think carefully about what talks you could give that would engage readers and make them gasp, laugh, and question the normal way of things.

3. I've spoken about the history of Dundee and Scotland and how that has shaped some of my books.

4. How about talking about the strange places your research has taken you. Seriously, I could deliver a whole workshop on that one. As a crime writer, I can see a dead body under every bush or behind every dodgy door.

HERE ARE some ideas for different genres:

Paranormal

1. Talk about haunted buildings in your area.
2. Hold a book signing in a haunted house.
3. Dress up as a character from Ghostbusters.

Romance

1. Despite my previous views on Valentine's Day, this is an obvious choice. Hold your launch on that day or talk about the history of Valentine's Day. This could be a fascinating talk.
2. Why not actually talk about St. Valentine himself and how it went from a martyred saint to a day celebrating love.
3. Cut out hearts and give them to your readers. Write sayings on them about love.
4. Hold a cream tea and launch your book there.
5. Give everyone who attends a little packet of love hearts. Who isn't a sucker for a love heart? And if nothing else, it will remind them of their childhood. Nostalgia is a great way of selling books. Remind them of the good old days.

HISTORICAL

1. Hold your launch in a historical landmark in your area. In Dundee we have houses, castles, ships, old mills – the possibilities are endless. Research what is available in your area.
2. Give a talk on the history of your town or the area where the book is set.
3. Dress up as a character from your book.
4. Talk about an aspect of life from the historical era in which your book is set.

CHILDREN'S BOOKS

1. Take props – I have stuffed animals from my *Bertie the Buffalo* Picture Books – Bertie, Ari the Alpaca, Hezzie the Buffalo and a bear. From *The Dagger's Curse*, I have a replica Egyptian dagger. I might add, the police have given me permission to use this and it is in no way sharp. Using weapons can get you into really serious hot water in the UK.
2. I am doing numerous book signings in the USA. For this, Bertie the Buffalo has a kilt. Again, this can be tied into social media with pictures of Bertie in his kilt used before and during the trip.

These are just some ideas of the top of my head. You can probably think of numerous others which fit your genre.

. . .

Since my first launch, I have undertaken a number of launches in Waterstones Bookshop. These have been well attended and the store have been pleased with how they have gone. It is important to ensure that each launch is as successful as the one before and to make sure you approach them professionally. You also need to ensure that you approach them with as much enthusiasm as you did previously. If you are enjoying yourself then so will everyone else.

If it is not possible for you to have a launch at a bookshop, then you will need to think of equally exciting opportunities. There is no rule that you have to hold a book launch in a book shop. How about church halls, village halls, theatres, libraries, school halls, coffee shops, craft shops or restaurants? In fact, anywhere that has the space to take you. If your book is set in a castle, why not approach a local castle and ask if you can hold your launch there. I appreciate that might be tricky, if you do not know the owner, but nothing ventured nothing gained. I brainstormed a few ideas for book launches and came up with these:

- Historical – As I said previously, why not have a cream tea.
- Crime - Hold a murder mystery dinner party for charity and launch your book there. I have actually done this and it worked extremely well.
- Sci Fi - Dress up as your favourite character.
- Romance - dress up as a romantic heroine or hero from the movies, or a book of course.

AN AUTHOR FRIEND OF MINE, Fiona Veitch-Smith, wrote a mystery set between the wars. This was *The Jazz Files*, starring investigative reporter Poppy Denby. She dressed up in clothing from the time, as did many of the guests. Her launch went with a swing in more ways than one. This is a great example of how to make use of your book's topic to build a buzzing book launch.

ONLINE BOOK LAUNCH

These are approached slightly differently and are mostly, but not exclusively, for ebooks. In my previous marketing book, I said that most authors set up an event on Facebook and invited people from their Facebook friends to join the event. However, the times they are a changing, and there are now many alternatives. I have outlined several of these below. These allow for a more immersive, interactive experience and are more akin to the real thing. Often your friends will invite other people and I would strongly advise you to encourage them to do so. The more people who know about the event, the more likely you are to have a full house on the day.

BEFORE THE DAY AND TIME, you post about the event everywhere you can, utilising social media to its full extent as well as informing fans via your newsletter, getting readers hyped up and ready. Choose a time when your guests are available. If you want this to be international, then remember the time differences. It may need to be later in the evening in the UK to accommodate guests from the USA. My advice, as per the previous chapter, is to start simple. Once you have done one event and it is successful then you can build this up.

. . .

YOU WILL NEED to prepare your plan in advance in order to ensure you have enough to keep the party lively. Like the real thing, you can offer food and drink, in a virtual sense of course, and make it fun. Name your cocktails after characters in your books or go with the theme of your book. Anyone for a Killer Cocktail? This goes with the theme of my books which all have the word Killer in the title, all having second word beginning with C. Remember what I said about branding a couple of times already in this book. Keep your brand in readers' minds. If you're a romance writer, anyone for a Smoochie Smoothie. Okay maybe my attempt at romance is a little off but you get the idea. As a romance author, you should be able to come up with ideas at the drop of your very beautiful heroine's hat. SciFi writer, these cocktails are out of this world or Cosmic Connection – readers and books, it's meant to be. Remember my ideas are a springboard for your much more creative and appropriate ideas. You know your genre inside out and what will attract readers of that genre. Although, I must admit, I am having a great deal of fun thinking about the different genres. Who knew there actually is a cocktail called a zombie, although ,with four types of rim, one of which is 151-proof, you probably will wake up feeling like the undead.

READ small extracts from your book and give the talk you would do if you were holding your launch in a venue where everyone is meeting up in the physical sense.

. . .

FINALLY, if you do decide to hold a competition keep the prizes small and light so they can be posted easily. Make it clear where you are willing to send the prizes. If you are in the UK it can cost a lot of money to send something to Australia or the USA. However, do not forget those readers, as it is now much easier to send ebooks than it was previously.

YOU SHOULD ALSO PROVIDE the opportunity for those attending the virtual launch to buy signed copies of the launch book as well as your back catalogue.

TOP TIPS for an Online Book Launch

1. Set a time and let everyone know when you will be going live. Start the buzz early get people excited about the event. Get readers talking about the event in advance. You can set up an Event Page on Facebook to get the word out even further.
2. Choose the time well, taking into account time zones. The best time for any online or virtual meetings seems to be 8 pm. That is 8 pm GMT/BST. This allows for most time zones to join in.
3. Consider taking out a Facebook ad in order to spread the message of the event further. This is especially valuable if you are launching a non-fiction book, but it can work for fiction as well. See this as a time to grow your audience and

therefore your readership. The world is, quite literally, your oyster for an online event.

4. Make sure sound is good and everyone can hear, before starting. If you are using Zoom, mute all of the audience. Sound checks will let you know if there is any feedback. If the session is being recorded, you need to check it is working in advance and be sure to speak clearly. Also, slow your voice down slightly. I have a tendency to get faster when I'm excited and, trust me, an online book launch is exciting.

5. Other alternatives to Zoom are Microsoft Teams, Skype and Facebook Live. Whichever one you choose, make sure you are confident in its use. Practice in advance with only yourself in the room if necessary.

6. Before the launch, prepare the area. You can have your other books in the background but your new book should be prominently on display. Preferably, many copies of your launch book. Try to keep the light on your face rather than behind you. Enter the online room early and check the lighting out.

7. For the launch itself, read from your book and give an interesting talk around the subject of the book. Keep the talk snappy, informative, and valuable. This is equally as important if your book is fiction or non-fiction. However, remember timing. People's attention spans are less online when other things compete for their attention.

8. Take real life questions from the audience as well as having some queued up in advance.

9. Keep it relaxed and fun. Attendees are there to enjoy themselves. This isn't a seminar. As writers, we often use digital media for writing and marketing talks – forget that style. Include humour, refer to the names of those who are attending. You can get some people to join in by asking them to unmute themselves. However, you might want to warn them in advance. People tend to seize up when caught unawares, especially when online.

10. 45-minutes is the optimum time as attention spans may start to drift after that.

11. Make sure you put the links in the chat for attendees to buy the books both electronically and also signed copies. Make sure to use universal links such as those from Books2Read which go to any digital bookstore. Update the bookshop on your website where readers can buy signed copies. Very often we are thinking of everything else and our own websites go out of our mind.

12. You might want to sign one copy of the book on air for dramatic effect and allowing for it to be as close to the real thing as possible.

Digital Launch

Increasingly, books are being launched with no physical or online presence at all. This makes use of all the digital technology and paid advertising to get the word out about your book and make it go with a bang. This does involve money but can be lucrative in terms of both ranking in the digital stores and in financial terms, if handled correctly. I am going to go into paid advertising in detail later in the book, but this technique makes full use of something called ad stacking which I will also discuss more fully later. Suffice to say, it involves using numerous platforms simultaneously to get the word out about your book and launching at a low price to get your book into the hands of as many readers as possible. One thing to remember is that low price will eat into your profit, but handled well, can lead to a good ROI.

IF THIS IS something which interests you, and you are about to launch your book, you may want to go to the chapter on paid advertising now.

EXERCISE

1. Jot down as many ideas as you can for book launches.
2. Research bookshops to approach for a launch.
3. Speak to the bookshops and discuss the possibility of a launch.
4. Jot down ideas for fun activities for an online event.
5. Set up an online event, allowing you to include readers from around the world rather than just your physical location.

7

WEBSITE

As I said earlier in the book website platforms can be either free or paid. The free ones include: Wix, Joomla, Wordpress, mailchimp, and Squarespace.

BEFORE I DISCUSS THESE FURTHER, I have one huge caveat. Since the first version of my book came out, data protection has, quite rightly, made an appearance. So, make sure whatever platform you choose, it allows you to follow smart security protocols. You will see the ones I have outlined above all use, htpps, the S standing for secure. This lets anyone clicking on your site know that security measures are in place.

WIX IS an easy to use drag and drop website builder. There are numerous free themes you can choose to help you set up a professional looking website quickly and easily. You can start simply with these and they will walk you through all the stages needed in order to build and develop your website. I have used Wix and had a simple website up and running in a couple of hours. Joomla and WordPress can be a bit trickier to use but are both excellent website builders. You can also get paid themes and options from all of these sites. Remember, websites are a long-term marketing strategy, so you need to consider longevity. You may start with one of the free websites and then discover they have limited capacity and do not meet your needs in the long-term. Having looked at all the options, I made the decision that WordPress allowed me greater flexibility and long-term sustainability. Since the first edition of this book came out, I have changed themes four times and I am currently using a paid for divi theme, allowing me to make more complex changes. At the time of writing this book, mailchimp are offering free website and custom domain for five years. This is a good offer but it is worth enquiring as to what the ongoing costs are likely to be.

You will also need to use a host service. This is the server where the website will sit on the Internet. I use Bluehost, which I have found to be excellent, but there are numerous others available. Do a web search for 'Top Ten Website Hosting Companies' and compare these for price and services. There is a cost for this each year as you are effectively renting web space. The cost per year is usually less if you pay for up to ten years in advance. However, weigh up the pros and cons of doing so. You may want the flexibility of moving before the ten years are up. At the time of writing as well as Bluehost, GoDaddy, HostPapa, and Hostinger are also popular options. Please note, I am not an affiliate for any of these sites, so make no money out of recommending them.

. . .

IT IS one hundred percent worth buying your own domain name. This is the name by which your website will be known. My domain name is wendyhjones.com which makes my website https://www.wendyhjones.com It makes sense to use your author name as this is the name you want associated with your books. I have known authors who called their website after their first book. Although this may sound like a savvy marketing strategy, it will lose its effectiveness once you have released several books. It could serve merely to confuse readers, rather than entice them to buy your books. You always need to be thinking of the long game when it comes to your website and, indeed, marketing.

ANSWER THESE QUESTIONS:

1. What is your five-year plan for your writing?
2. What is your five-year plan for your marketing?

A WEBSITE IS one of the few things which you, personally, control when it comes to marketing. Even if every social media site dropped off the face of the earth, you can still advertise and promote books on your website. Even if every bookshop, real and virtual, disappeared, you can still sell books from your website. This is why it is worth investing both time and money into building it and to making it the best showcase for your work.

. . .

PLEASE NOTE, if you are in the UK and wish to sell digital products from your website, you need to be clear about the legal aspects of VAT. However, should you wish to do so, use an online shop such as Selz, Payhip or Shopify. I use Shopify as it was already available as a plugin as part of my paid website theme. So far, I am only selling paperback copies of my books from my website, as I didn't want to get involved with the VAT aspects of selling books. At the time of writing, the UK has decided there will no longer be any VAT on ebooks to bring them in line with VAT on paperbacks. Whilst this is extremely good news for UK books sales, remember, there is still tax on any books you sell in other countries; therefore, I would still advise you to use one of the digital shopfronts outlined above. I am not a lawyer or a tax advisor, so I would strongly suggest you get advice on this from an expert.

UNLESS YOU ARE a computer whizz kid, it may be better to hand the website building over to someone else. I am fairly computer savvy and it took me quite a number of hours to get to grips with website design. A website is considered a marketing essential but your time may be better spent on writing more books.

IF YOU DO WISH to design your own website, there are a number of excellent books which will help you master this. I am not going to recommend any specific book as the one you buy will be dependent on your level of skill at the starting block. Also, as you will be well aware, the digital world changes so quickly. My recommendation would be to buy the most up to date one available at the time of reading this book.

YOUR WEBSITE SHOULD CONTAIN, as a minimum:

1. Your newsletter sign-up - This can be a popup or static but it should be on your landing page, as well as every other page. I will be talking about this in greater detail in Chapter 8. However, this is one of the most important parts of your website. Taken together, your website and mailing list are the two most powerful marketing tools you own.
2. A strong Author Bio – this is not a CV, so should be interesting and tell the reader something about you as a person as well as you as a writer.
3. Links to buy personalised signed copies of your books. I sell a lot of books this way as people buy signed copies as gifts.
4. Links to buy your books from Amazon, Apple Books, Kobo, and Google Play. Please note, there are also a number of other digital stores available and your books should be available there, but too many buttons on your actual website may put people off. Obviously, the choice is yours as to which you include - one of the business decisions you will need to make.
5. Social media share buttons – this allows your readers to share your news, books, photos and other aspects of your website. It is all part of building a buzz. Encourage your readers to share. Social sharing is gold dust to an author's career.

6. Follow buttons to your social media profiles – Remember, the more readers see you and your books, the more likely they are to buy. The more places they follow you, the more invested they become in you as a writer and, by default, your books.

7. A page for your blog – the jury is out on whether blogs have relevance today, as video is becoming more prominent. However, I have one as it allows me to engage with more people and provides a platform where I can support other writers.

8. Embedded book previews from Amazon where visitors to your site can preview the books and then buy directly from Amazon. I have also added links to all the other booksellers where my books can be purchased. Whilst Amazon is a major player in the book world, I sell books across all platforms.

9. Your Twitter Feed - This allows others to see you as more than just a writer. It lifts you from 2D to 3D proving that you have a life other than writing. It also provides instant access for visitors to any promo posts you may do on that platform.

10. A link to Instagram. At the time of writing, this is one of the fastest growing social media sites and, as I said previously, is outstripping even established sites such as Pinterest.

MAKE the most of your website. It is a powerful tool in your Marketing arsenal, containing everything about you in one easily accessible place at the click of a mouse.

. . .

ONE OF THE most important things to remember when building your website, is the rise and domination of mobile technology. More people are now using mobile devices than desktops or laptops, to browse the Internet. In January 2019, it was generally reported that 52% of users accessed the internet via mobile phone, an increase of 10% over 2018. By April 2020 it was generally reported that this had grown to between 53% and 55%. It is interesting to note that the use of tablets appears to be declining and I have, just this week, got rid of my iPad and moved over to using my iPhone for everything. My iPad was sitting in a corner, gathering dust. For months. Growth in mobile use is phenomenal in African countries in particular. It pays to be at the forefront of mobile technology and to keep up to date with these trends. You want to be able to tap into the emerging markets, many of whom are only using mobile. Young people are also, more and more, turning to mobile use only. My nieces, and their friends, only use mobile. The eighteen-year-old does not have a computer at all. The fifteen-year-old only uses hers for graphic design and multi-player online gaming. The world is changing, so you need to make sure you are changing alongside the world. If you want readers to know about your books you need to ensure that you are accessible on the technology which they are likely to be using. Your website has to be mobile friendly.

I WOULD LIKE to take me as another example. Whilst I use my laptop and desktop for work, I use my phone for virtually everything else.

. . .

ANOTHER IMPORTANT POINT of note is, Google, and other search engines, will also give greater placement in the rankings to websites which are mobile optimised. This means it is worth spending time and money to make sure your website is fully mobile compatible. Once it has been built, and after you make any changes, check it out on multiple devices to make sure that all pages are loading properly and quickly. Also, check this again at regular intervals. Issues may arise with future updates. I cannot stress highly enough how important this is.

IF YOU ARE LOOKING for a web designer, there are two designers I can highly recommend. They are highly professional, customer focussed ,and will build an outstanding website which will fully meet your needs.

ALAN WHITEFIELD OF ONLINE CREATION. Despite the fact the website says Cheshire and Merseyside, they can work globally. The website link is https://onlinecreation.co.uk/

COLIN EDWARDS OF CREATIX CMS. Again, despite the website saying Lincolnshire, Colin works with customers worldwide. The website link is https://creatixcms.co.uk

BOTH ALAN and Colin have experience working with authors and will either build a website from scratch or help and advise you through the process of building your own website. Please note, they will not teach you how to build a website, so if you go for the help and advice option, you will need some basic knowledge of web building and design.

<u>Exercise</u>

1. Analyse the websites of seven authors who write in your genre. It may also be worth comparing the websites of authors in other genres.
2. How do the different genres compare? What do they have in common?
3. What do you like about them?
4. What don't you like about them?
5. Jot down some ideas for your own website.
6. Write a plan for your website. What do you want to include as a basic minimum? What would you like to include if you had an unlimited budget?
7. If you already have a website, plan changes which will show you and your work in a better light.

Make sure your website portrays you as both a professional and a serious writer. Unless you are writing about fluffy bunnies, you might not want them cavorting around your website. You may think I am being a bit too over the top with my warning. I certainly don't want you to think I am being overly dictatorial but, trust me, I have seen websites which are completely wrong for the image they are trying to portray.

8

GOING WIDE

This is simple. Your book should be available on every platform to which you have access. This means in every bookshop, as well as every online retailer. Let me walk you through this.

Bookshops

Obviously, we are talking paperbacks here. I will cover ebooks later in the chapter. You may be thinking this is easy, if my book is out there, bookshops can get it. You'd think so but, in many ways, this is not the case. In order for your paperback to be ordered by a bookshop it first requires an ISBN number and needs to be registered on Nielsen. You also need a method of distributing your books to that bookshop. Let me break this down into all the individual components

. . .

ISBN Numbers

For those who may not know, ISBN stands for International Standard Book Number. This is the number which appears on the barcode on the back of any paperback or hardback book. In the UK you get these from Nielsen. Every country has their own ISBN provider and you must buy them from the country where you reside and run your publishing business. The costs in the UK. At the time of going to print, are as follows:

1 Single ISBN £89.00
Block of 10 £164.00
Block of 100 £369.00
Block of 1000 £949.00

Initially, I bought a block of 10 but I have now bought a block of 100. This brings the cost per book down considerably. The 1000 option is likely to be for publishers or highly prolific writers.

But I can get free ISBN's from Amazon and Ingram, why should I pay for them? It's a good question. The answer lies in the fact that the ISBN belongs to the publisher, not the author. Therefore, if you get free ISBN's from either of those companies, they will be the publisher of record. If you are independently, rather than traditionally, publishing your books, you want to be the publisher of record for those titles. This means you retain total control over the books and can publish them wherever you want. If you have an

Amazon ISBN for your book, the likelihood of any book-shop stocking your book, or allowing you to do a book signing is somewhere in the region of zero. If you want to independently publish your book, then own your book from A to ISBN.

Distribution

Amazon can work as a distributer if you enable expanded distribution. My advice would be to avoid this and use Ingram Spark for expanded distribution. This advice is for those who self or independently publish as distribution is handled by the publisher. I would like to unpack this further. Ingram Spark has a wider reach when it comes to distribution. They distribute in more countries and most bookshops will stock your book more readily. I say most, as some bookshops may not have an account with Ingram Spark. However, Ingram do feed your book's data to Nielsen. This means your book is available almost every-where. One caveat. Also, add your book to Amazon, other-wise that retail giant will say out of stock, available in about 6 weeks, despite the fact they will arrive much more quickly. Ingram are print on demand, so if a reader orders your book from the shop, the order will be printed immediately in Ingram's facility, in the country in which they buy the book, and will immediately be sent to the shop to fulfil the order. It's magical.

ONCE YOU HAVE COMPLETED THIS, your book will also show as available in the online catalogues of Waterstones in the UK, Barnes and Noble, and Books a Million in the USA, Chapters Indigo in Canada, and Dymocks in Australia etc.

So, it really is available everywhere. Here I am in Scotland, knowing someone in the USA or Australia can order my book. I have also recently been shown images of my books in bookstores in Finland and Estonia. Ingram's reach is wide.

INGRAM ALSO OFFER advance catalogues for books printed through them. Ingram has 3 Advance catalogues: One that is 1) general purpose and two others that are focused on 2) Children's and 3) Christian. All three are used to make a one-time announcement of a publisher's current/forthcoming book. The catalogue is delivered to Ingram's retail and library customers. You can pay to have your book advertised in this catalogue, which is distributed to bookstores worldwide. I was involved in one catalogue where my book was the front cover. You can't pay extra to go on the front cover, it is down to Ingram who choose the images to fit the particular catalogue at any given time.

eBOOKS AND DIGITAL Retailers

WHEN THINKING of digital eBook providers, everyone's thoughts turn to Amazon, the leading digital book provider, with their Kindle books and readers. However, there are so many more online retailers who can distribute your book to a wider audience. You are probably wondering why I am rattling on about publishing when this is a marketing book. Bear with me, I promise it's relevant.

. . .

LET'S tackle the major player first - Amazon. The biggest decision to make is, do you put your book into Kindle Unlimited or KDP Select as it is known for authors. For anyone who doesn't know, Kindle Unlimited is a subscription model, where readers pay a certain amount each month and can download as many books as they want, as long as the book is enrolled in Kindle Unlimited. The author is then paid a certain amount for each page read. Whilst I don't know how much it will be when you read this book, at present it is somewhere in the region of 0.004 cents per page read. You will obviously get more if the reader finishes your book, than you would if they give up part way through.

THE BENEFITS of enrolling in KDP Select, and this is where marketing comes in, is that you can do special promotions offering a free book, in order to garner new readers. Whilst it may be counter intuitive to give your book a way for free, it can be useful for a first in series to drive sales of the next books in the series. There are also Kindle Unlimited countdowns where the book increases in price over a period of a few days and Amazon will say in the pricing that it goes back to X price in Y days. This is to entice people to buy whilst the price is reduced. This can be a good marketing strategy but there are two things to consider:

1. Once in KDP Select, you will be contracted to remain there for 90-days before you can leave.
2. During that 90-days you will not be reaching an audience on any other retailers' platform. This means you are losing sales via these retailers.
3. You are at the mercy of one company. Whatever

they decide happens to your book during this time, you have little control over.

4. Your books will not be eligible for the digital library catalogues.

5. Once you come out of KDP Select, you will need to start from zero building up visibility on Amazon and every other store.

THEREFORE, there is a strong argument for going wide and using all the platforms that are available. These are numerous but the main ones are:

- Apple Books (Formerly iBooks)
- Kobo
- Nook
- Google Play
- Barnes and Noble
- Scribd (ebook and audiobook subscription service)

OTHERS INCLUDE, 24 Symbols, Playster, Angus and Robertson (Australia), Indigo (Canada), Mondadori Store (Italy), Bold (Germany).

YOU'RE PROBABLY THINKING, *I haven't got time to get my books into all those stores.* You would be right. There is a way to do it with little effort. If you upload your books to an ebook aggregator such as Draft2Digital they will be distributed to many digital stores. However, there are a couple of caveats. Isn't there always.

1. Always use KDP or KDP print to get your books into the Amazon Stores.
2. As this is a marketing book, if you want to use the paid marketing campaigns run by Apple Books or Kobo, you will need to publish your books directly with them.

In order to be fair, I need to say that there are other book aggregators available. These include Smashwords, Reedsy, Publish Drive, and even Ingram Spark amongst many others. I have found Draft2Digital extremely easy to use but it is worth exploring your options.

I THINK this is a good time to mention Universal Book Links. These are links which you can use to direct readers of your ebooks to the store of their choice, based on the country in which they buy their books. So, one link for all stores. Universal Book Link providers include

- booklinker (Amazon only)
- Books2Read (all stores)
- BKLNK (Amazon only but also has numerous other cool features for authors)

I HAVE USED all three of these, so I know that they work well and are worth using.

· · ·

<u>Exercise</u>

1. In your notebook do a Pros and Cons list of going exclusive to Amazon. Then repeat this for going wide. Which model is best suited to your business?
2. Explore Ingram Spark's Website. Read the resources and take notes. Look at the countries where they distribute.
3. Compare three different aggregators and choose the one that best suits your business.
4. Compare the Universal Link Tools and make links using at least one of them.

9

BOOK PROMOTIONS

This chapter will be covering physical book promotions. Online book promotions will be covered in greater detail later in the book.

PROMOTING your book can be hard work, but it can also be lots of fun. My experience is that the fun far outweighs the hard work aspect of promotion. You also get to meet a variety of readers, some of whom will buy your book, some who won't. That doesn't matter. They are seeing your books and may buy in the future. They may also tell family and friends about your books. Not everyone will read in your particular genre, but they will know others who do.

BELOW ARE a number of places where you can do book signings:

Cafes
Shopping centres

Coffee shops
Craft Fairs
Christmas Fairs
Book Fairs
Summer Fetes
Schools - Yes, I write crime fiction. However, I was asked if I would like them to sell my books to the parents and donate £1 from each sale to the School funds. I have also done events at schools with my children's books, usually around the time of World Book Day or during Book Week Scotland. This is with both my children's books and my adult books.
Fund raising events - give a proportion of each sale to the charity
Conferences
Libraries
Museums
Re-enactment events - particularly useful if you write historical fiction

WHILST THESE ARE PRIMARILY about selling books, they can be so much more than that. They are also about promoting your book. On your table you should have postcards for each of your books with the book cover on the front and the blurb and buy links on the back. You can take this one step further and add a QR code. Scanning this will take them directly to the site to buy the book. If visitors say they only read on an ereader, then give them the postcards. The same applies if they say they don't read crime. They may have friends or family who do, so will take the cards. Book signings are as much about promoting as selling. They are also about building up relationships. I find that when readers get to know you, they are more likely to buy into you as an author and, subsequently, your books.

TRY to make your table set up as visually appealing as possible. If you just have books, it is human nature to think *They're trying to sell me something* and many people will scurry past. Make it appealing and they will stop to chat. When I set out my table, I have books (of course), postcards, bullets, a dagger (replica and I have permission from the police to use it), syringes (pens not the real McCoy) and a hangman's noose. More about that noose later. I also have some free sweets to give away. The sweets are my secret weapon. If you ask people if they would like a sweet it serves two purposes

1. They notice you.
2. They usually stop and chat.

This can be particularly true if you are in coffee shops or cafes. If you are sitting at a table with a pile of books many people will walk past. If you ask if they would like a sweet they will take notice. I have many people say to me, "I didn't even see you there. What are you doing?" They have then gone on to buy one or more books. Never underestimate the power of a free Quality Street when considering marketing. By the way, I use Quality Street because they are gluten free. Any other wrapped sweet will do.

ALONG WITH YOUR table being visually appealing it is sometimes worth dressing up yourself. I have done book promotions as Jack the Ripper and Santa Claus. I will admit the Santa outfit was basically a Christmas jumper and a Santa hat. My spiel, "This is your only chance to get your crime book signed by a smiling Santa." I change this to Jack the Ripper for other signings. For the *Fergus and Flora Mysteries* I dress up as an Ancient Egyptian as *The Dagger's Curse* takes place in ancient Egypt as well as contemporary Dundee. I have a Bertie the Buffalo hat and t-shirt for the *Bertie the Buffalo* books. Some ideas for you could be a suffragette, or the hero or heroine from your book if they are distinctive enough. This may also give you more confidence to engage with visitors as the eyes move from you selling books, to your display. Selling books is a pleasant aside to the whole event.

ANOTHER WRITER FRIEND OF MINE, Dorothy Stewart, wrote a superb book called *When the Boats Come Home*. This was a historical saga based around the fisher women who followed the herring boats around the country. For one event she dressed up as a fisherwoman. However, Dorothy took this one step further and learned how to gut herring. Now that is what I call dedication and genius. Genius marketing that is. What could you do that is different and will get you noticed?

ANY EVENTS you do should be well advertised. Put up posters, hand out leaflets, and discuss with the venues how they will promote it. Talking of venues, many are more supportive of writers than you would think. Go in, tell them you're a local author, say why it is linked to that particular venue and ask if you can do a book signing. The worst they can say is no. If they say yes, set a date and time. If they say no, try another venue. I haven't had a venue say no to me as yet. Most are keen as it can bring in extra custom. Also, use social media to advertise your event. Tweet about it using an appropriate hashtag. There will be more about hashtags in Chapter 12. Set up a Facebook event and invite people along. When I do an event, I also tweet about it and stream to Facebook, live from the event. This reminds people that the event is on and may also reach new readers.

ANOTHER METHOD OF PROMOTION, which is quick, and relatively cheap, is to carry postcards around with you. Hand these out if anyone asks about your books. I buy these from Vistaprint, but there are many other places where they can be purchased. You may also be able to get them locally and support a local business. Ask local businesses and cafes if you can leave postcards in there. Many are happy to support local enterprises and that is what you are.

GOING BACK to what was said at the beginning of the book, a customer needs to see something 6 or 7 times before they buy. Therefore, you need to make sure that you are in as many places as possible. This does not mean you personally but includes that. It means posters, flyers, events, postcards, bookmarks and anything else you can think of which will get the word out about you and your books.

ONE FUN IDEA I use is t-shirts. Some authors have these with their book cover on. Mine merely say:

'Anything you say may be taken down and used in a book'

'You are dangerously close to becoming a body in my next novel'

These make people laugh and start a conversation about your books. They can also be worn at book signings as, again, they will start conversations.

I do have one shirt with the book cover on it and that is for Bertie the Buffalo. I wear this for events where I am reading Bertie the Buffalo and the children love it.

IN MANY CASES there will be an initial outlay for book signings. Coffee shops and cafes will usually allow you to do signings for free. I usually buy a coffee or some food. However, tables at Craft Stalls will cost money upfront. As a rough guide I pay £10- £15 per table depending on where the event is being held. Promotional materials such as postcards also cost money. You will also need to buy paperbacks in order to have stock to sell. You should consider this as an investment in your business. You need to make the decision if your business, in this case your books, are worth that investment. I have made the decision to say a firm yes to this, as I want readers to be able to find my books.

PROMOTIONS ARE about getting to know people and them getting to know you and your books. Chat to people in general. If someone says they are buying a book for a birthday present, ask them if they would like it signed Happy Birthday or something else. Tell them about your books, but if they say they don't read crime, don't force it. Ask what types of books they do read and chat about that. They will remember how pleasant you were and might buy your book for someone else when a present buying occasion comes along.

. . .

MY TOP TIP when attending book signings at craft fairs or any other event:

Arrive early and set up before it starts. Do not start to pack up until the end of the event. I have had people buy all six of my books in one series whilst other stalls were still setting up. I have also sold copies of every book I have written, to one person, just before I packed up. If you say you will be there for a specified length of time, then you must be there at that time.

EXERCISE

1. Jot down a list of places you could approach to arrange book signings.

2. Choose 3 of these and approach them today.

3. Research places where you could have postcards made and work out the costs.

4. Jot down a list of local businesses who you think would be willing to take postcards or flyers.

10

FREE PROMOTIONS

There are a number of ways that you can promote your books for free.

AS AN AUTHOR you may find that you are a member of several organisations. If you are a member of an organisation use their benefits and services wisely. They provide help, support and access to a number of experts in both writing and publishing. Many of you may be members of the Society of Authors. This includes those of you who are traditionally and independently published. Independent and hybrid authors may also be a member of ALLi (The Alliance of Independent Authors). I am a member of ACW (The Association of Christian Writers), in fact I am their webmaster at the time of writing this book. I am also a member of the Scottish Fellowship of Christian Writers. My books are not in the slightest Christian, but I am a Christian so eligible for membership of these organisations. I am also a member of SCBWI (Society of Children's Book Writers and Illustrators), Sisters in Crime and The Crime Writers of

Canada. Each of these provides links to your work on their websites - your books, blogs, websites and often events. The Society of Authors and ALLi have search functions to discover authors to do talks etc.. Of course, these organisations provide so much more than just advertising your book. However, as this is a marketing book, I will be focussing on the marketing aspect.

I SUGGEST that you use these organisations to their fullest if you are a member. If you are not a member, then it is well worth exploring membership. The links to these can be found at the end of this chapter.

THIS IS one for Scottish Authors only – apologies to the rest of the world. If you are an author in Scotland, then you should apply to be included in the Scottish Book Trust Live Literature Database. Not only is this a way for event organisers to find authors as speakers, but also a means of getting funds to pay the author. Any Live Literature events you undertake you will be paid. If you are traditionally published applying to be included on the database is fairly seamless. If you are independently published, the process is a little more complex and slightly longer. Either way, it is well worth applying. I have had requests to attend numerous events through this database, especially during Book Week Scotland, as well as launching the Summer Reading Challenges for Both Dundee Libraries and Angus Libraries.

. . .

BOTH ALLI and ACW have a blog, which comes out daily. There are opportunities to be guest bloggers or even regular contributors. This will be covered in greater detail in Chapter II on blogging. Again, this is effectively free advertising and a way for you to get your name known in the wider world. However, it is also about supporting others, by providing information that will be of benefit to other authors and readers. Make the most of these opportunities. They are like gold dust.

JOINING online groups for your specific genre, or country, is also a good way of getting the word out about new releases. I am not saying everyone in the group will buy your book, but they do tend to be supportive. They will also share with others. Please note, like all interaction, these groups are not about 'buy my book'. Their primary function is to support members with writing and to celebrate achievements. Look out for online writers' groups and join them. Interact and engage long before you start to tell people about your books. As with everything, engagement is the key to selling more books. Once people know you as a person, they are more likely to buy or share your books. Be generous. Be nice. Support others and basically act like the good person I know you are. If people then support you in return, consider that a bonus. If they don't, it's their drama, not yours.

YOU CAN GET free advertising for your events via local newspaper websites. These publications often have free listings for local events in the print version of their newspapers as well. Talking of newspapers, it is worth sending out a press release to local and national newspapers. They may publish you, or they may not. This may bring sales, or it may not. Opinion is divided as to how effective newspaper articles really are. However, it is another way of getting your name out there. Remember that a customer needs to see a product at least six or seven times before investing in the purchase. It is worth having a press release kit ready to send out to newspapers. This should contain:

Your author bio:
1. Information about your book.
2. The release date of the book if it is a new release.
3. A high resolution, professional photo of yourself.
4. A high-resolution image of the book cover.
5. You can also add some sample questions and answers as they may use these as the basis of an interview

LOCAL RADIO INTERVIEWS can also help to get your name out to the wider public. Listen to your local radio and identify the programme which has the best fit. This is important as you want to have the best chance of getting airtime. Contact the DJ and outline what you do and how it will benefit local listeners. Let them know you are available for interview. Sending them a copy of the book will give them a better idea of how you fit into their programme. Be polite and pleasant. If you are accepted for interview, then take time to prepare. Learn about the show. Listen to several episodes. Learn something about the person interviewing you. This way you will come across as a pleasant and all-round person rather than someone who simply wants to flog their books.

. . .

THINK about other media opportunities as well. I contacted STV, the Scottish version of ITV. For those of you not in the UK, this is a television company. They weren't able to interview me for the main news, but they did do an interview for STV online and have continued to do so as each book comes out. These have been viewed and shared a number of times and is getting the word out about my books.

EXERCISE

ONE EXERCISE only for this one. Jot down ideas for places you can get free promotions. Approach these places and see what comes of it. Yes, it really is time to step out of your comfort zone.

11

MAILING LISTS

Along with your website, your mailing list is one of the few things you can totally control. If every other method of marketing fell apart, you would still be able to use your mailing list. Of course, if the world's electricity supply died tomorrow, it might be slightly trickier. However, that's a story for another day, and I can feel a novel coming on.

BACK TO OUR MAILING LISTS. As I stated previously, it is important that you have a sign up for this on your website. It can be either a popup or a static signup; what is most important is that it is mobile friendly. Many people now are doing their entire web browsing on mobile devices. As of July 2020, mobile internet traffic globally is 50.44%. In the USA mobile share of digital minutes is 77% (Statista online). These are staggering statistics. If it does not show up on a mobile, then vast swathes of the world's population will not be able to see it. It is worth employing a professional for this part alone, even if you design the remainder of the site yourself. I know this from experience. In my first marketing book, I shared that I was able to add the signup myself and then discovered it would only open on a computer or a laptop. I had to call in the big guns to sort it out. Since then, I have moved over to a new mail provider (more of this later), the process was much more simple, and the signup worked seamlessly on all devices. Mail providers are ensuring their products meet the needs of the modern user. As many people have popup blocker installed on their mobile devices it is worth having both a popup and a static signup. Delay the popup so it does not interfere with what they are reading straight away. Readers need time to invest in the content of your website before being interrupted by a popup.

One of the best ways to get someone to sign up to your website is to give them something free in return for their email address. As a writer, it makes sense if this is a book. I have written a new book for this purpose, but it fits in with overall series image and branding. In my books there is a running theme where DI Shona McKenzie is thinking about ways to kill her boss. Many people said they liked this aspect of the book and found it funny. Therefore, my free book is *DI Shona McKenzie's Guide to Killing Your Boss*. It is a PDF file and can be read on any device including mobile devices. Whilst I have numerous books out at the time of writing, I have not chosen to give away the first book in my series. I know many other authors who do. If you are a veteran writer with a lot of books under your belt, then this may be something worth exploring. I may do this as my portfolio grows, but at the moment the only way to get the book I am giving away is to sign up to my newsletter.

. . .

OF COURSE, that works brilliantly but what of my non-fiction books and the *Writing and Marketing Coach* side of my business? Anyone who signs up to my writing and marketing newsletter gets a free writer's toolkit.

You may be thinking, *I don't have time for any of this*. I agree it does seem somewhat daunting. However, you can start off simple and go from there. I know authors who have started by giving away a short story. Rather than being put off by the perceived enormity of the task, see it as an opportunity to expand your business. Remember, I said way back at the beginning you need to be willing to change your thinking.

THE WORDING of the signup needs to entice the reader to buy the book. I have the following on my website

'Shona is feisty, funny, sharp and smart. She also spends a lot of time thinking about how to bump off her boss. Here for the first time she shares her secrets with you in the free book, *DI Shona McKenzie's Guide to Killing Your Boss*.'

Under this are fields for name and email address then a clickable button saying, 'tell me where to send your free ebook now'. However, one important point to remember. Since the advent of GDPR, you must make it clear that anyone completing the form is signing up to a newsletter in return for the free book.

Give the reader a taste of what they are getting, but keep it simple. Remember those mobile readers. The more information they have to wade through the less likely they are to click through. Click through is the name of the game when considering email sign up.

. . .

ONCE YOU HAVE AN EMAIL LIST, it is worth advertising it to grow it. This will be covered in more depth in chapter 12. You also need to ensure that you send out quality information. This can be about what you are writing, interesting facts about the location where your book is set, information about the characters, writing hints and tips, discussions about books, and last but not least, letting followers know about future book releases. Keep it short, keep it lively, and keep it interesting. Readers now have many demands on their time. If they have to spend half an hour reading your email letter, then they will not carry on. Especially if this is on a mobile device. However, it is important to make it long enough that you engage the reader. Try it out, see what works, and make changes if necessary. The beauty of this is the flexibility. If it doesn't work, change it until you find out what does work. Each time you try it more readers will sign up.

WHEN IT COMES TO NEWSLETTERS, you will be sending this out via email. The subject line of your email is crucial. The average person in the western world has hundreds of emails dropping into their inbox on a daily basis. The important factor is click through. That is, how many people are clicking on your email and opening it. The title needs to catch the eye, and imagination, if subscribers are to explore further. There are a number of blogs and articles out there which will help you to examine this in more detail.

You should run your email list through email handling software such as mailchimp, Aweber or mailerlite, amongst many others. This handles all the legal stuff like keeping addresses private and not spamming people. It allows you to add an unsubscribe option at the bottom of the email, which is a necessity under GDPR rules. Most importantly, it automatically adds anyone who signs up, to the relevant list and makes it not only easy, but quick, to send out multiple emails. It also gives you data such as number of subscribers and number of click throughs. When I first set up my list. I used the free version of mailchimp which was then good for up to 2000 subscribers. However, not only did this not have many of the automated features that make it much easier to use, they also reduced the subscriber number for the free version. I then moved to the paid version which was much more versatile. However, there has been a further development since the first version of this book.

Mailchimp, although still an excellent company, expanded the marketing and web design aspect of their business. I was increasingly finding the functionality I needed from the mailing list side to be difficult to use. Nor was I able, without a great deal of technical help from their support team, to segment my list. I am willing to own, that may be an issue with me, rather than mailchimp, but I felt it was a good time to explore other options. I therefore moved my list over to mailerlite. This was a seamless process with no break in service whatsoever between providers. The steps below were simple and mostly the same whether you are migrating your list or setting up a new list.

1. Download your list from mailchimp.
2. Add the mailerlite signup form to your website.
3. I use Wordpress for my website and this was an easy matter of downloading the mailerlite Signup Form widget to my website.
4. Add the API key that you will receive from mailerlite.
5. Develop a form in your mailerlite account. This

is a simple matter of clicking on forms and
following the instructions.

6. The minimum information you should collect is
   name and email address. I also added a nice
   image of the free book I was giving away. I used
   Bookbrush to produce the image but more of
   that later.

7. Back in Wordpress, click on add form created in
   mailerlite.

8. Click on create form.

9. Upload your mailing list to mailerlite and then
   within seconds you will have a nice new mailing
   list.

Do remember, however, that you need to be comfortable
with any list you use. There are subtle differences and
nuances between each provider.

Whichever you choose, I would advise you to have a
strong onboarding sequence. This means writing a series
of emails which will go out automatically after someone
signs up. For my novels I have a series of five emails as
follows:

1. Your free book. - This is triggered once someone
   clicks the confirmation email to say they have
   agreed to be on the list. This provides a link to
   somewhere they can download the free book. It
   also lets them know how often they can expect to
   receive newsletters from me.

2. Did you enjoy your book? – This provides some
   background to the main character and provides a
   link to download book one in the series at a
   special price.

3. Another great offer. – This one gives some information about book two in the series
4. Thank you for joining my author journey. – This paints a picture of me as an author, talks about the rest of the books in the series. It also invites readers to join me on social media.
5. From the Cradle to the Grave. – This is where I introduce my other series and explain that I have books that can cover all age groups.

By this point, subscribers are beginning to get to know you as both an author and a person and will be invested in you and your books.

One of the most useful benefits that you get by using these services is the data they collect. I can see that 72% of subscribers to my list have subscribed via a mobile device. That is almost three quarters of readers who are interested in my books. With statistics like this, you can see that it is imperative to make sure that any mailing list activity is fully mobile compatible.

Once you have built your list, you can use campaigns to send out a regular newsletter or contact your subscribers with news of new releases or events. The important part here is not to spam your list. Use your list wisely and provide benefit to your subscribers. Use your list to turn casual readers into loyal fans.

Some people use the lure of large prizes, such as a Kindle, to entice readers into signing up for their mailing list. This is false economy and will probably not result in a lot of sales. People will join in the hope of winning the prize and will not be invested in your books. They will probably unsubscribe soon after the competition closes. Mailing lists are about gaining fans, not the largest number of subscribers. It is quality over quantity. If you give away a free book, and if readers like it, they will stay signed up to your list and may buy more of your books.

Once you have your email list up and running, it is important that you send emails on a regular basis. This should be the frequency you stated in the initial emails. Make these interesting – it's not all about buy my books. For non-fiction, these should be informative and helpful, preferably related to the subject matter in your books. That doesn't mean they can't also be personal. As an example, for this book, I could talk about some of the strangest things I have done to promote my books or the strangest places I have signed books. In my case, I have signed books in the crypt of a castle, during *Crime at the Castle*, a crime festival I co-founded. An alternative is to talk about when something went wrong and how you dealt with it. Be human, and don't be afraid to make it fun – the readers will relate to you more fully.

Exercises

1. Explore both of the above email management companies.
2. Decide what you could use as a free gift to encourage readers to sign up for your newsletter.
3. Choose one and sign up to the free trial today.
4. Do you feel it suits your needs? If so, start building your email list now.
5. Work out an onboarding sequence of four emails.
6. Brainstorm topics you can use for your first twenty emails. Once you have these, the task won't seem quite so daunting.

12

BLOGS

Every writer should have his or her own blog – although the jury is out as to whether that is still the case. My take on it - this is another area of marketing totally under your control. Remember what I said about a reader needing to see you and your books six or seven times before they will invest in you/it. This is another example of a way in which you can connect with readers or potential readers. If you haven't already got a blog, then there are some free blogging platforms to get you started. These can be integrated into your website once this is up and running.

Free Blog Hosting Sites:
Blogger
WordPress
Wix
Squarespace
Weebly
Jimdo
Squarespace

I FIND blogger the easiest to get up and running; you will need to decide which is the best for your needs. Recently, Blogger have had a major revamp, and everything is looking a lot different. Many people are saying it has lost functionality, but I have not found that to be the case. In the interests of fairness, I have not used the others (I only use Wordpress for my website.), so I cannot compare them or come down hard on any version.

THE FREE VERSIONS of these sites can a have a few limitations, but they have enough features for you to have a professional blog up and running within minutes. You can choose from a number of professional themes, and I am confident you will find one which reflects your business brand.

ONE POINT TO NOTE, if you are thinking of having a Word-Press website, then it may be better to have a WordPress blog. This is not essential; I have WordPress/Blogger, but it may make things easier down the line.

HINTS AND TIPS **for bloggers**

1. Any blog with a number in the title usually gets the most views. This is proven fact as people like to know what they will be learning or getting from reading the blog.

2. Maintain focus but write on diverse topics within this. For example, a writer's blog could contain - author interviews, tips on writing, technology for writing, technology for readers, book reviews, short stories, and book launches among many others. You could also share marketing tips and photos of book signings or book launches. This is a good example of how all marketing works together.

3. Disseminate your blog. This is not the time to hide your light under a bushel. People won't read it if they don't know it's there.

4. Use pictures in your blogs. Blogs which contain pictures are more likely to be read and shared. Many people are now sharing on Pinterest and this cannot be done without a picture.

5. In order for your blog to gain followers you must:
Write well.
Write often - this does not mean every day unless you want to. However, if you decide to write once a week, then keep to the schedule. Readers will lose interest if there are gaps.

6. You can use your blog for marketing your own products. Be careful not to spam. Treat it like you would any social exchange. Social media, of which a blog is a part, should be 90% social 10% product information. It is perfectly acceptable to put permanent links to your books on the side of the blog. When I say social, in terms of blogs, this can also include articles about the business of writing and/or marketing books.

7. Link to your blog on your website. You want to point people towards your website wherever possible.

8. Add share buttons for Facebook, Twitter, Pinterest, Instagram, and TikTok etc.

9. Remember your blog is a showcase for you as a writer. People who read your blog are more likely to buy your books, especially if what you are sharing in your blog has perceived value.

10. Add a call to action, such as a question which can be answered in the comments. The more interaction there is on the blog the more fun it will be for readers. It will also be more discoverable in online searches. Discoverability is key in all aspects of marketing.

YOUR BLOG CAN BE USED to showcase your new book releases and is a valid part of your marketing plan.

BLOGGING IS SO MUCH MORE than writing your own blog and sending it out into the stratosphere. It is also about reading blogs on writing and marketing and keeping up with what is new in the industry. Here are a few which I particularly like:

Social Media Examiner https://www.socialmediaexaminer.com
Writer Access http://www.writeraccess.com/blog/
The Creative Penn https://www.thecreativepenn.com/blog/
Jane Friedman https://www.janefriedman.com/blog/

The first one is not specifically about marketing books, but it is excellent, and all the advice is transferable.

BLOGGING IS SO MUCH MORE than putting out your own blog. It is also about social sharing and supporting others. One of the ways in which you can do this is to host other writers or marketers on your blog. This can be in the form of interviews or guest posting. Look out for opportunities to guest post on other blogs within the industry. Very often these will come along when you are not looking and you will be invited to another blog. These opportunities are golden and you should, wherever possible, grab them with open arms. However, make sure that you are a fit for the blog in the first place. It isn't worth going on a blog about quantum physics if you've written a children's book. Unless your book is about quantum physics for children of course. Okay, I'm being slightly tongue in cheek here, but you get the picture.

Some requests can be quirky but a perfect fit. I absolutely love the following example. I was invited to guest post on Shelley Workinger's fabulous FoodFare blog. This is about food in fiction. My post was on the food they eat in my *DI Shona McKenzie Mystery* series. Anyone who has read my books will know that Shona and her team eat - a lot. What an exciting opportunity and what a great idea for a blog. If you would like to take a look at Shelley's blog here it is http://bookfare.blogspot.co.uk. One word of caution, writing a quality blog can take up valuable writing time. It is useful to weigh up the pro's and con's if you are being asked to write too many. It's a balance between getting the word out and it becoming a time suck.

. . .

BOOK REVIEW BLOGS are also a good way of getting your work known. There are many of these and they do an amazing job. However, review bloggers are often booked up months in advance. Look for some of these in your genre and reach out. It is important to make sure that the blog is the right fit for your genre. An excellent one for crime writers is Lyndsey Adams *There's been a Murder* blog https://theresbeenamurder. wordpress.com

LOVE BOOKS GROUP also do paid blog tours. At the time of writing it costs £100 for the organization plus you are expected to give a free book to the bloggers if they review your book, so you need to factor in the cost of the books plus postage. These are extremely well organised, and I have had some fabulous reviews. Please note these are reviews on the blog and they may not translate to Amazon. Some will also be posted on Goodreads. I have been able to use quotes from the blogs in my social media and on Amazon. With regards to sales of the books, this is difficult to measure as the analytics are out-with your control. You will need to make a business decision as to whether a paid blog tour is something you would like to get behind. As I say, I have had several successful tours.

EXERCISE

1. Spend a few minutes looking at reviews of the different blogging platforms.
2. Jot down ideas for the main focus of your blog. Brain-

storm some titles and do a search to see if these are already taken.

3. Set aside a couple of hours in your diary to get your blog up and running and write your first blog.

4. Research blogs that you think will be a good fit for your books. Reach out to ask if they would either allow you to do a guest blog or would be willing to review your book.

13

SOCIAL MEDIA

This section could be turned into a book on its own. In fact, Chris Syme has done just that in her book *SMART Social Media for Authors,* which I would highly recommend. This chapter will give you a brief overview of the ones I use regularly. It will also suggest some ways in which you can use these effectively to start your own social media marketing quickly and easily.

THERE ARE a large number of social media sites out there, and I mean a *large* number. The latest list I could find outlined 176 different sites. *Influencer Marketing Hub* suggests that in 2020 we should know 75 of these. I took a quick look through and there are many which are niche and even more of which I had never heard. It is obvious that no author, especially one who actually wants to write books, has time to worry about 75 social media sites. You might be thinking *not a chance* as you read these, and I wouldn't blame you. However, it is important to be on at least some. The main ones are Facebook, Twitter, Pinterest, Linkedin, and Instagram. TikTok, a Japanese video sharing platform is growing extremely rapidly. I have to say, I have not been able to get to grips with TikTok, and I feel it is for a much younger demographic than me. However, an industry expert I was speaking to recently suggested that TikTok could be a useful platform for authors using video to expand their reach.

IT IS advisable to be active on at least four of these. If you write Young Adult books, then I would recommend Snap-Chat as this is the site used by those in that age range. YouTube is also extremely popular amongst teenagers. Even if you do not want to be on any of these at the moment, I would advise you to register your author names on each of the sites. If your author name has already gone, you need to think carefully about what you will use as an alternative. It needs to be professional and allow readers to find you. I was fortunate in that I registered for the sites I use pretty much as they started out. I was also fortunate in that I used my middle initial on these sites long before I started writing. This means my author name was already registered. I am telling you this because it may be as simple as adding your middle initial. You may need some lateral thinking here to come up with a solution.

GOING BACK to my statement about fluffy bunnies in the website section, unless you are literally writing about fluffy bunnies, using FluffyBunny101 as your username may not be the smartest move. I'm not treating you like an idiot here; I am using this as an extreme example to emphasise a point. Often, users will choose a name other than their own, to preserve anonymity. However, this seriously impacts on discoverability. Using your author name means two things:

1. Your social media will come up in internet searches.
2. Anyone typing your name into a social media search will find you quickly and easily.

Why make it difficult when you can make it simple?

THE MOST IMPORTANT thing to remember when considering social media is that it is called social, and not selling, media for a reason. It is designed to interact with friends, family, and fans not flog your books or courses. The balance should be 90% social and 10% about buying books. Long gone are the days where writers could hide behind a screen of anonymity whilst they sat in the proverbial garret and wrote their magnum opus. Fans now expect to be able to interact and get to know more about the authors whose books they enjoy reading. You may not wish to share your life with fans, and for you, it will fall into the SWOT threat category. However, seeing it as an opportunity can turn this around. What can you share without giving away every intimate detail down to inside leg measurement? I share things about the weather (I'm British, we can't go five minutes without talking about this topic.) but make it funny. I share humorous stories, post photos of where I am, and what I am doing, and generally make my profile a fun place to be.

SOCIAL MEDIA MARKETING can be fun. In fact, I would go as far as to say it should be fun. It is an opportunity: for engagement and conversation, for inspiring and informing, for learning and for teaching, for celebrating and commiserating. I could go on. As you can see, it is so much more than selling books. It is about being you, and you will sell books as part of the process. Don't be so desperate to flog your books that you forget you are, first and foremost, a unique and exciting person who also happens to write books. As writers, we are so caught up in our writing identity, we can often forget the rest of our lives.

Social Media Sites

Facebook

I AM sure you will already be familiar with Facebook. Essentially, it is a free social networking site where you can connect with friends and upload video, pictures, and links. You can share news and chat with others with whom you are friends. Make it an enjoyable experience where others want to hang out. Family, friends, and readers will then want to join you there and will interact with your posts. Interaction is vitally important, and you will find out why in a minute. As far as writing and marketing goes, there are two ways in which you can interact with readers.

FACEBOOK AUTHOR PAGE

. . .

IF YOU ARE RUNNING A BUSINESS, you are not allowed to do so from your normal Facebook profile. If Facebook finds out you are doing this, they will remove your profile without discussion. You will then lose all the contacts and friends you had made prior to this happening. They are strict on this and will give no notice before removing your profile. Therefore, you must have an Facebook Author Page. You can call this what you want, but a simple name followed by author will suffice. Remember it must be a page not a profile.

YOUR AUTHOR PAGE is the place to share news about books, events, cover reveals, new releases, your newsletter, courses etc.. However, it is still a place where you have to be social. On my author page, I share pictures about what I have been doing both work related and social. I also share interesting facts and photos of Dundee, the setting for my books. For example, I shared the BBC news item of a theft of a cash (ATM) machine from a shop nearby. The police then caught the thieves at a nearby McDonalds. This was merely a bit of light relief. I have also shared pictures from the Scottish Association of Writers Gala dinner, at their conference. Pictures from *Bloody Scotland* have also been posted and shared. Who can resist a few photos from a conference with a name like that? It is a crime conference, by the way, before you think I am slagging off my homeland. I also use my Facebook page to upload videos of book launches and to do Facebook Live streaming of events.

WHEN IT COMES to your author page, interaction is the name of the game. The more likes and comments your posts get, the more people will get to see your posts. Only about 4% of those following your page will see your posts organically. Facebook is a business and, like all businesses, want to make money. Therefore, they want you to advertise to boost your posts. Facebook advertising will be covered in greater detail in chapter 13. I would not recommend that you pay to boost posts but use advertising itself for anything important. More advice on that later.

FACEBOOK GROUPS ARE ALSO a good way of getting the word out about your books as well as being a great way to find new authors and new books to read. Like everything, interaction is the name of the game. When you join a group, take time to interact and get to know other members. If you do post about your book, check back and respond to any questions or comments. Let's think about the equivalent in the real world. Would you go into a group, hand out flyers about your books, talk about your books, and nothing else, then walk out of the door without letting anyone get a word in edgeways. This is effectively what you do if you dump and run in a Facebook group. However, one caveat, do not thank everyone who likes your post. This bumps your book up to the top of the group page again and is considered bad manners. Use groups wisely. Do not post the same thing to a hundred groups in one day. This will just clog up your friends' notifications and they will lose the will to live or at least the will to remain friends with you on Facebook. There are also a number of groups which are purely for learning and supporting each other. These are superb and worth their weight in gold. I am a member of several of these and have learnt so much from other writers. The most useful one I have found is that belonging to the Alliance of Independent Authors. (In order to be a member of the Alli group you need to be a member of Alli itself. It is worth joining Alli for this group alone, although there are also so many other benefits.).

There is usually a no promoting your book rule in these groups, and I fully support that stance. If a group is about education and support, using it just to post your books is extremely bad form.

ONE OF THE ways in which I use Facebook, and indeed all my social media platforms, is to show pictures of my books on bookshop shelves, myself at book launches, book promotions and signings, or anything else to do with your book. These go down well and are a good way of getting the word out about your books without saying buy my books. They should, however, be interspersed with social sharing.

FACEBOOK LIVE IS AN EXTREMELY easy way to livestream events. Please note, this has to be done from your phone. It's a simple matter of:

1. Go to the page group or event you want to live stream to.
2. Tap live at the bottom of the post composer.
3. If you want, you can add a description and tag friends you think might be interested.
4. Tap – start live video.
5. Do your talk, book launch, afternoon tea party, or whatever you want to live stream.
6. Answer any questions that come in whilst you are live. It is often better to have someone

holding your phone so they can mention some of the people who have joined and also ask the questions that have come in. This makes it more interactive and enjoyable for the audience.

7. Tap finish.
8. The video will then stay on your feed for anyone to watch after the event.

If you want to do it from your computer, you can do so using a platform called StreamYard. You can also share to Facebook Live via Zoom, using this platform. One of the advantages of using a platform such as StreamYard is that you can invite members of the audience onto the stream and they can answer the questions live. Limited space in this book means I can't go into the ins and outs of StreamYard but do check it out.

ONE ASPECT of social media marketing which must be addressed is post reach. I am sure many of you know what this means, but as a refresher or for those who don't, this basically means the number of unique people Facebook allows to see your content or post. There are different types of reach depending on the post.

1. Organic – this is the number of people who see your post without you paying for the privilege.
2. Shared (or viral) – This is the numbers of people who see your post after it is shared by others.
3. Paid – this is where you pay to boost a post or pay for a Facebook Ad.

ORGANIC REACH IS DECREASING ALL the time as Facebook put checks and measures in place. They say they have done this to ensure that only quality content is shared and that content meets the needs of Facebook users. You will find if you share a link, your reach will decrease even further. The cynic in me says this is because Facebook wants you to pay for advertising space. However, Facebook is a company and they need to make money, so one cannot blame them. It is, after all, a free to use platform. One way to increase your organic reach is by sharing content that people want to read and that they like. This is where interaction comes into play. The more interaction you have on a post, the more Facebook will increase your organic reach. The likes and, more crucially, comments tell Facebook that your content is popular. Therefore, two points are key.

1. Share content that you know people will like.
2. Respond to all, or most, of the comments that are left.
3. Comment on other people's posts to give them a lift. You cannot expect people to comment on your post if you totally ignore, or only like theirs.
4. It can also help to be the first to comment on your post.

A minor point about sharing posts. It makes more sense if you say why you are sharing. Merely sharing a book that has come out or on promo doesn't say to your fans why you think it was important to share. If you say, my author friend Joe Blogs has a book out today and I know it's going to be cracking, then others will be more likely to buy into the post that Joe Blogs has written.

. . .

PAID reach will be covered in the chapter on Social Media Advertising.

FROM MY PERSPECTIVE, I have found that posts with images are extremely popular and get a lot of interaction. Memes are also popular, but with everything, it is worth shaking things up. All images, or all memes can quickly become wearing. Variety is the name of the game.

TWITTER

I AM sure that many of you reading this book are already using Twitter and are familiar with the site. For anyone new to this, Twitter is a microblogging site where you have 280 characters to impart your deepest thoughts in a tweet (post). In my previous marketing book, the character limit was 140 so it has doubled. This does not mean you have to use all of the characters, shorter tweets can often be more effective, so it is worth playing around with the length to see what the sweet spot is for interaction and sharing. Your tweet can then be retweeted (shared) and liked by others. The idea is that you follow people and read their tweets. These often contain links which can take you to articles, author websites, places to buy books or other items, or any other site on the World Wide Web. They often have photos attached or the aforementioned memes. You can use this site to get the word out about new releases, reduced price books, 'cover reveals' or any other photo which you feel will be of interest to your followers.

. . .

WHEN STARTING ON TWITTER, many people do not grasp how it works or how useful it can be. This is because they are following few others and have no followers themselves. As a writer, start by looking for other writers in your genre and follow them. Then you will get an idea of how it is generally used by authors. However, Twitter is so much more than that. You can follow people with many different interests and tastes. Follow people who may be writing about the areas you need to research for your novels. Send out tweets yourself and make them interesting and informative and people will start to follow you back. This is when it starts to get interesting.

IN ORDER TO USE TWITTER, you need a Twitter Handle. This is how people will be able to find you. Funnily enough mine is @WendyHJones. My advice is to use your author name unless it is already taken. If it is, think again, but remember not to be too weird and wonderful. If you want people to find you and see you as a professional writer, @FluffyBunny may not give the right impression.

HASHTAGS ARE ALSO important when using Twitter. A HashTag is the symbol # followed by a word which then signifies the topic of your tweet. Anyone searching for that HashTag will see your tweet. If you are looking for Hash-Tags to market your books, blogs etc. then here are some, which I have found useful. As a guide you should use no more than two hashags per tweet.

#Iamwriting

#Amwriting

#Writing

#Editing

#1lineWed (one line from your book with book link - it works)

#Writingwednesday

#AmEditing

#AmReading

#WritingTips

#writinginspiration

#writingprompt

#writerslife

#readingispower

#author

#authornews

#booklaunch

#poets

#poetry

THIS IS JUST a quick guide to help you get started. However, I would be doing you a disservice if I did not mention two more hashtags:

#WritingCommunity

#Writerslift

These are designed to encourage interaction between writers on Twitter and if used correctly, can be a powerful way of getting the message out about you and your books. When I say, used correctly, take time to follow the hashtags and see how they work and interact with them, re-tweeting and responding to other writers' tweets. Then you will get known as someone who is helpful and supportive. Then, other writers will be more likely to support you.

THERE ARE many tweet groups where authors band together to retweet each other. These can be good, but use them sparingly and use discretion. If you never mention diet or food in your tweets, and the only books you mention are crime, your followers are going to wonder why you are suddenly tweeting about a book on the cucumber method of dieting. Okay, I made that up, but it is usually obvious you are a member of a tweet cartel. You do not want to put your followers off, as they will start to unfollow you. Like everything, relevancy is key to how you interact on Twitter.

FOLLOWING ON FROM THIS, you will also see posts saying put your Facebook page/Twitter handle/ Instagram link in the comments and we'll all follow each other. This is not a good idea on many fronts:

1. You only want people following you who are interested in you as an author and your books. Having 20,000 followers and only 500 who are actually interested in you, is not the best business move.
2. Remember, the social media platforms are throttling your reach. What if the only people who ever see your posts are the ones who followed but are not interested?
3. Interaction will be poor from those false followers.

In other words, make sure that your followers are genuine and interested.

SOCIAL MEDIA CAN BE a time suck and authors often find that they spend far too much time on there. In frustration ,they start to automate everything they do. My advice is do not do this. If you follow someone on Twitter and they immediately send you a private message saying thanks for the follow here's a link to my book, website, Amazon author page or Facebook page, this is a sure indication they are using an automated service. If you do this, then you will find yourself losing followers faster than you can say unfollow. Please do not use automated services.

TWITTER CHAT

THIS IS another excellent use of Twitter. I have been involved in a few of these and I have organized one myself. This can be a really good way of interacting with fans and other writers those interested in your genre. There are few simple steps before doing so.

1. Find two or three other authors in your genre, and invite them to join the chat.

2. Arrange a date and time when you are all free. Remember to allow a few days to advertise the event. If you want to chat to an international audience, then you need to remember the time differences. The one I did was at 9 PM GMT. This allowed readers and writers in the USA to join in the chat.

3. Advertise the event widely using social media. All

writers who are involved should contribute to the advertising.

4. Where possible advertise using graphics as this will catch the attention.

5. Make sure you communicate clearly with all those taking part. Tell them when you expect them to be available for the start of the event.

YOU CAN TAKE this even further. Why not have a prize for the winner of the best question in order to ensure there is a lot of interaction. You can give a signed copy of one book from each of the authors. You could then then ask the winner to post pictures of themselves with the books on social media. This leads to increased advertising for the books.

#Pitmad

#Pitmad is a Twitter event where writers can tweet a 280-character pitch for an unpublished manuscript. Agents and editors will follow this feed and like any that they would like to follow up on. These happen on a specific date at a specific time in March, June, September, and December, so it is worth keeping an eye out for these.

YOU CAN ALSO ADVERTISE on Twitter and again this will be covered in chapter 13.

Pinterest

· · ·

THIS IS BASICALLY a way of pinning photos and articles on online pin boards. Other users can either follow you or each of your individual boards. These can be about anything you want them to be. I have a number of Pinterest boards including - Social Media Marketing, Writing, Books and Reading. Mystery Writing, Forensics, Literary Quotes, Gluten Free Food, Penguins, My Dundee, Scone Palace, and Stirling amongst many others. Yes, you've got it. Pinterest is all about social sharing and being supportive of others. You can share other people's pins and people will follow you if you pin things which are of interest to them. They will also repin your pins. "So how can Pinterest help me to market," I hear you ask? There are a number of ways in which this can be done.

BOOK BOARD - just for your books, covers, links to buy, interesting articles about the area in which they are set, and interesting articles about the period in which your books are set. An example of this would be pictures of clothes set in the time period of your book. This is particularly suited to Historical Fiction, but a little bit of thought will mean you can use this for any time period.

INTEREST BOARDS - If your character rides a Harley Davidson then a board on Harley Davidsons would be perfect. Any boards which would be of interest to your readers. So, if you are writing romance book start a board about Valentine's Day or romantic Christmas gestures. I write crime, hence the reason I have a forensics board.

. . .

BOOK LINK BOARDS - These could contain the pages of all your books on every platform on which they are available. This should be the only specifically buy my books board you should have.

YOU CAN HAVE secret boards which you and only those invited can see. Now before you think I am suggesting anything dodgy here, I am not. I have a secret board only I can see. In there I keep research for my books. My cover designer and I also have a secret board for sharing possible cover images.

AGAIN, you can pay to promote on Pinterest. I have dabbled in this but I'm not sure of how effective it is for books, so I will not be concentrating on Pinterest advertising.

Instagram

INSTAGRAM IS A PHOTO SHARING APP. This is one which you mainly use on your phone as it is designed to be instant sharing – so, take the photo on your phone, then share. You can make your account public or private. However, if you are using it to get the word out about your books, making it private doesn't make a great deal of sense. Unless you are a mega celebrity, the name of the game is following others and having them follow you in equal measure. These can be friends, family, celebrities, readers, other writers – much the same as all the other platforms. To get you started with Instagram, you can use the discover page for suggestions of who to follow. Follow a few people and let others know you are now on Instagram in order that you can follow each other. It can be a slow process building up a following on Instagram and over a thousand followers is considered a healthy number. When you post, you comment on the image. If you also ask questions, this will increase your engagement which will mean, like all the other platforms, your reach will be greater. You can also use hashtags liberally on Instagram. Apparently, the sweet spot is 11 hashtags. The great thing about Instagram is, if you start typing, they will give you numerous hashtags to choose from, which saves a lot of time. One point of note. Any links you put into Instagram will not be live links and it appears to be impossible to copy and paste them. So, the best move is to change the link in your bio and say 'link in bio' in your comment.

STORIES

No, this is not another platform but a new aspect of both Facebook and Instagram. Stories are a different way of getting your message out. The images are vertical and you can add text and stickers to them. They stay in the story section for 24 hours and when someone interacts with them, the comment comes via messenger or messages in the case of Instagram. The beauty of these is that, at the time of writing this book, there is no throttling of the reach for stories on either of those platforms. Obviously, this may change in the future. It pays to make full use of these while the going is good.

. . .

As you can see there are a diverse number of ways in which you can use social media effectively. This is, on the whole, free advertising, so use it well. Don't waste the opportunity by spamming everyone on your friends list. Use it to have fun, enjoy yourself, and entertain and support others. In the process, you will sell books.

Posts with images usually get a lot more engagement on social media. There are two programmes I use to create promotional graphics for my books - Canva and BookBrush. Even those who, like me, are graphically challenged can produce fabulous images. There are free versions of both, but I pay for BookBrush as it has much greater functionality.

Exercise

1. If you are new to social media register your author name on the five major ones.
2. If you are already using social media, use some others which you could use to develop your social media marketing.
3. Connect with others in your field on the different social media sites.
4. Look out for Twitter chats and join in the conversation. This will help you to get your name out there as someone who is supportive and interested.
5. If you have been using Twitter for some time, identify a couple of authors and invite them to join in a Twitter chat.

14

PAID ADVERTISING

Much of what I have been advising so far is free or low cost. However, if you are serious about selling more books, then you will, at some point, have to use paid advertising. There are a number of sites which offer paid advertising. This can cost anything from a few dollars to thousands of dollars. I can't tell you which ones to use or guarantee they will work for you. However, I will outline a few of these so that you can explore them further. You need to make the decision as to how much you are willing or able to spend on paid advertising.

BookBub

This is the platinum level of advertising. The number of subscribers varies from 200,000 to over 3,5 million depending on the genre you write.

. . .

THERE ARE two types of advertising on BookBub.

1. Featured deal – these are curated by BookBub
staff to ensure a carefully selected range of books
targeted by category. The costs vary depending
on genre. As a crime writer it informs me there
are 3.5 million subscribers and I could expect
2.960 paid downloads. However, they do not
guarantee this and the advertising costs at the
time of this book going to print are $782 for a free
book - $3984 for a book which costs $3 and up.
This is if your deal is served to all regions. This
cost drops if you advertise to selected regions.
The USA is still high with the cost being topped
at $3,066. The top cost for international is $918
but with expected paid sales of 710. I know this is
a lot of money and a significant investment for
most authors yet, I do know authors who have
had good returns from this and have sold
thousands of books. However, as I say, this is not
guaranteed. I have not been successful getting a
BookBub featured deal yet, but I fully intend to
continue trying. Please note, not all books put
forward for a place on BookBub will be accepted.
I know numerous authors who have tried several
times to get accepted for a featured deal but have
not yet been successful. The key here is to keep
trying. BookBub themselves say to keep
submitting after the required time period
between requests has lapsed.

2. BookBub ads – You can run an ad campaign for
any book you choose on a cost per click model.
You decide the readers you want to target, how

much you want to pay per click, you overall ad spend and finally the length of your campaign. Your ad goes into an auction with other authors and when a reader opens an ad, they are served the ad of the highest bidder targeting that reader. It is a lot less complex than you think and BookBub have some great tutorials to help you with this.

3. Featured new releases – These are curated like the featured deals and are designed to drive full price sales. The price for a deal is $920 in my genre of crime, but this can vary significantly depending on genre.

Books Go Social/The Book Promoter

THIS IS an excellent company run by Laurence O'Bryan. They offer a number of different promotions at various price points including, Twitter campaigns, featured author deals, daily newsletter promotions, Net Galley review services, paid Facebook, and Amazon Ad services and placement in their Amazon store. In order to see the full range of services they offer, and prices, go to https://bgsauthors.com/pricing/.

I HAVE BEEN IMPRESSED by any promotions I have booked with them and have been extremely pleased with their responsiveness and professionalism.

. . .

I WOULD HIGHLY RECOMMEND this company for advertising. However, remember that sales cannot be guaranteed with any promotion that you do.

EREADER NEWS TODAY (ENT)

THIS IS A WELL-ESTABLISHED company and is highly recommended by many authors. Again, prices vary with genre and the price of the book you are advertising. However, the most you will pay is $150 at the time of this book going to print. They do have a large number of subscribers and their email list is popular with readers. You can submit books up to $3 but they say the greatest results are seen at free and $0.99. I have done a promotion with them with a book at $1.99 for their featured book of the day and saw a healthy return on my investment.

THE FUSSY LIBRARIAN

THIS IS ANOTHER WELL-ESTABLISHED SITE. They have around 124,000 subscribers and will add you to their newsletter on the date of your choosing. Weekends can be booked up months in advance. They give clear guidelines on what is required, and it is easy to apply. There are two services:

1. Bargain books – you will be expected to reduce the price of your books and these can be anything from $0.99 to $5.99. The most you will pay is $21 for genres such as fantasy, romantic

suspense, and women's fiction. Subscriber numbers vary depending on your genre but are all healthy numbers.

2. Free books – These cost more to advertise. This is usually used for a free first in series, where downloads are key to increase sales of the remainder of the books in a series.

I HAVE USED this service and I did notice a small increase in sales, which continued after the promotion finished. My read through rate also improved dramatically.

FIRE AND ICE Book Promos

THERE ARE different ways in which you can advertise on this site – 1-week, 14-days or 28-days. The costs at the time of going to print are $20, $30 and $40 respectively. It is worth taking a look at this package to see what it has to offer. Please note, at the time of this book going to print all books for the promotion need to be priced at $1.99 or below.

Book Cave

This is very carefully curated as the daily newsletter contains only one or two books. They review every book submitted and give it a rating like a film rating for content. Prices vary depending on genre with the maximum you will pay being $36. In the newsletter they will give the rating saying things like, some mild crudeness or moderate violence.

Free Booksy and Bargain Booksy

These pretty much do what they say on the tin – you can advertise bargain or free books. Prices start from $20 and go up to $75 depending on genre. You can also do deal of the day for your genre. My genre of thriller costs $120 for this, but other genres cost from $80 (science-fiction) to $195 (romance).

Before promoting your book on these sites, it will need reviews. If you haven't got a minimum of ten, then most sites will not accept you for promotion. Some require more. Your book also needs at least a 3.5-star review average on Amazon. Most book promotion sites require your book to be available on multiple platforms e.g. Amazon. iBooks, Kobo etc.. It also helps you to be accepted if you can be flexible with your timing. Make sure that you look at the requirements before submitting to make sure your book has the highest chance of being accepted.

These are just examples of the numerous paid advertising sites available. It is worth exploring others. A search on the internet will reveal many more. Before you go ahead with any paid promotion. check that they have the number of subscribers to their newsletters written down on their site. That way you can make an informed choice as to whether it is worth paying out money.

. . .

ADVERTISING ON SOCIAL Media

SOCIAL MEDIA SITES are all free to use, but as I indicated earlier, they are also businesses. This means they need to make money in other ways. In order to encourage users to take out ads for their posts, they throttle the reach of your posts. Advertising becomes the name of the game and this is how they make their money. Pay to play is becoming increasingly more important, a huge shift since my first marketing book came out.

Facebook

YOU MAY HAVE 2000 followers but only 4% of these will see any given post. This is the organic reach of your post. This is usually limited to people who have recently liked one of your posts so the same circle of people will be seeing each other's posts.

THIS MEANS that in order to expand your reach you will need to use paid advertising. There are three ways in which you can do this.

THE FIRST IS to **boost** an individual post. This can be done very cheaply depending on the number of people whom you would like to boost it to. This type of advertising merely shows the post to a larger number of people. It will contain a sponsored message.

In my first book I said that it was worth trying a boosted post. You may want to try this once as an experiment, using only a low-cost boost, on the whole it is better to avoid these. The reason for this is, the boost post is essentially an ad where Facebook decides the objective is greater engagement. This means you pay every time someone engages with the post, not for clicks to your links. So, you are literally paying for someone to comment or like your post rather than clicking on the link. There may be very few people who actually click the link to your website or through to buy the book.

THE MOST USEFUL method is a straight advert. This is more complex than the other method. You will develop your own ad using Ads Manager. The advantage of using this method over the others is that it looks like any other post in the newsfeed. It will be labled, promoted or sponsored, but will also have its own URL. This means people can buy your books, or go to your website, directly from the ad.

YOU WILL NEED to set a budget for how much per day you are willing to spend. It is advisable to start low, say $5 per day. Also set the number of days you would like the ad to run for. It is important to make sure you do this, or your costs could soon mount up. The important thing to realise and remember is that you are paying per click, not per number of people who buy the product. Therefore, it is easy to lose money using Facebook ads. You need to make the decision as to whether you are willing to take that chance.

· · ·

I HAVE USED Facebook advertising and have made a profit from my ads. However, I am not a Facebook ad expert; therefore, I am unable to give you advice as to how to run ads on the platform. Also, this would take a whole book in itself. If you are thinking of going down the advertising route, then I would recommend that you complete Mark Dawson's excellent online course - *Facebook Advertising for Authors*. This is not cheap, but it is worth the money to make sure that you are giving the ad its best chance of being seen. This takes you through the steps to make sure your advert is in the best place to receive click throughs and purchases.

In my previous books I talked about using Twitter advertising. Whilst this can still work for certain products, the perceived wisdom as I write this book, is that they don't work for books. Therefore, at this time I would not advise going down this route. However, the choice is yours and you may feel you want to experiment.

Amazon Ads

PLEASE NOTE, this is for independently published authors only. If you are traditionally published, then any ads must be run by your publisher.

IN MY PREVIOUS MARKETING BOOK, I did not even mention Amazon ads. However, these have become exponentially more important in the past four years and most professional authors are now using them. Before you start using these, you will need to do the following:

1. Go to Amazon Author Central. If you do not already have an Amazon Author Central account, then you will need to set one up.
2. In your author central account, set up a payment method.
3. Go to advertising.amazon.com and set up an account. This is the dashboard you will use to run your adverts.

An important point of note, Amazon ads take a lot of patience and tweaking. You may not see results for several weeks. I have made a small profit from running Amazon ads so far, but I am playing the long game. Amazon ads are not a quick fix but an exercise in learning how to do them properly and when and where to make changes.

AT THIS POINT, again, it would take a whole book to guide you through the process of setting up and running Amazon ads but there are solutions.

BRYAN COHEN'S free *5-Day Amazon Ad Challenge* which runs four times a year. This is an excellent starting point and will get you up and running. This feeds into a paid course which takes six months. However, you do not need to go on to the paid course.

MARK DAWSON also runs an Amazon ad course that, although expensive, is excellent.

. . .

THIS IS NOT an area where you want to go off and experiment. As I say, it takes knowledge, patience and, as you need to set up a lot of ads in order to get the process to work, time. So, my advice would be to invest in one of these courses if you have the money. It is one of those situations where it is worth the investment in your business.

PROMOTION STACKING

THIS IS the process of running several promotions simultaneously in order to get your book as high up the rankings as possible. This is usually done in connection with a special promotion price for your book. It can be run all together on one day or over a set period, say 3-7 days. In the past this meant booking slots with the various promotional sites, but this has expanded to include Amazon ads, Facebook ads, your newsletter, social media campaigns, and newsletter swaps. Obviously, this can cost a significant amount of money but you can see a return on your investment. Also, if you make it to the top of the Amazon charts, then this will give your book more exposure. Read through rates will also help.

EXERCISE

1. Block out half an hour of time in your diary.
2. Spend time exploring some of the different promotional sites.
3. Choose one and commit to taking out an advertising spot

15

THE POWER OF THE CROWD

This is also known as social sharing and this should never be underestimated. Facebook and Twitter encourage this with their share and retweet functions respectively. However, social sharing is also so much more than this. It is also:

1. Word of mouth as readers tell their friends about the fantastic book they have just read.

2. Reviews on Amazon and readers sharing those reviews.

3. Readers emailing friends and telling them that they have just got to read this book.

4. Fans telling their friends about your latest event on Facebook, Twitter, or any other social media site.

5. Fans posting on your author page about how much they enjoyed your book.

6. Contact from bloggers who would like to host you on their blogs.

7. These blogs being shared and read by a wider audience than you can reach alone.

8. Being interviewed on podcasts.

9. Being Interviewed on Facebook Live.
10. Attending virtual events online.

THE POWER of the crowd can expose you to many more potential readers and showcase you as a professional and well-respected writer.

HOWEVER, social sharing is not just about your own work being shared. It is important to be supportive of others and share their work where appropriate. This should not be done with any thought that you might get something in return, but because it is the right and pleasant thing to do. You should do it because you want to and you genuinely want to help others. I have found that most people are willing to help and support you in return. If they aren't just move on.

Social sharing can happen in a number of ways. For instance, one of my friends was recently in hospital. The person in the bed opposite was reading one of my books, and my friend started a conversation about knowing me. The person in the next bed then heard about the books and asked their relatives to buy a copy. Thus, conversations are born, and books are bought.

Here is another example of social sharing. I was doing a book signing in a shopping centre. I was setting up before the centre opened and one of the security guards came to chat to me. We had a conversation about the books, and she bought one. All day people were then coming along to my table and saying Vicky sent me over. She says your books are great. They then bought a book. All because of a friendly conversation with a security guard. I wasn't trying to sell her my books, as I hadn't yet unpacked them. Yet, the net result was I got several sales.

You are probably realising that social sharing cannot be bought. Yet, it is possibly the most powerful form of advertising that can be used. The power of the crowd is exponentially greater than all the individual sales you make. I can't advise you how to make this happen; I can only say be nice to people. Talk to them as people, not potential customers. Take an interest in them. They may buy then, they may buy in the future, or they may never buy. However, you can bet your bottom dollar they will be telling their friends they met an author and how friendly he/she was. This may be what gets you the sale. So, to reiterate – Be Nice.

Social sharing will come when you treat people as you would like to be treated yourself. Be supportive of other authors and engage with readers. This engagement does not mean answering every review you get on Amazon or anywhere else. In fact, I would advise you never to respond to Amazon reviews whether good or bad. They are one reader's perspective on your work and your book. They are entitled to review about that perspective no matter what their thoughts are.

Social sharing is also about the way you behave on social media. We all share our thoughts and feelings there daily. In fact, it is increasingly becoming a fact of life. I had a friend say as a joke – I forgot to tell Facebook I was in A&E, so it obviously didn't happen. Friends, family, fans and prospective fans can see these unless you have your account locked down tighter than the vaults in the Bank of England. They will make assumptions based on what you say. It is important to be positive in the way you come across. Even when handling criticisms in social media comments, remain polite and do not get into an argument. On the whole it is better to ignore negative or inflammatory comments rather than start a flame war. Handle yourself pleasantly and professionally at all times. I appreciate most authors reading this will already know, and act, like that. However, it can be so easy to react badly when faced with criticism.

ONE OF THE best ways to gain influence on social media is to start following others; share their posts, retweet their tweets, comment on blogs or their posts. They may then follow or friend you and a relationship can start to develop. One caveat - do not do this to the point of creepiness. This may get you noticed in the wrong way. Once you build up a relationship with others, they are more likely to be supportive of you and help you to share your posts and work.

HOWEVER, the power of the crowd is so much more than social sharing. It is also about working together with other authors. This can be done in a number of ways:

1. Joint book signings.
2. Joint speaking engagements.
3. Interviewing each other or hosting each other on blogs.
4. Providing support and advice.

IN CONJUNCTION WITH A LOCAL BOOKSHOP, I organised a four-author event called, Local Authors Live. Each author represented a different genre - crime, historical saga, young adult and children's. We spent four hours in the shop using a joint table for our books. During this time, we chatted with customers and told them about our books, and those of the other authors. This can work well if all the authors are invested in selling all of the books. It is quite a simple premise. When a customer approaches and starts to look at books, simply ask them what type of books they are looking for that day. They may be looking for a present for a grandchild or looking for a crime book to take on holiday with them. Authors should be prepared to talk about all the books placed on the tables. No one should be in competition with anyone else.

Joint author talks can also be fun. This can be in the form of a chat between two authors or the authors could question each other about their work. It is a matter of identifying another author and then agreeing on the process. However, remember the public are involved and their questions can be enlightening. I was once doing an event at a nursery and one of the questions I was asked was, "Have you ever been to the airport in your pyjamas?" All I can say is, be prepared for anything.

EXERCISE

1. Identify one key influencer in your genre on one social media site.
2. Read their posts and follow their page or tweets. Observe how they interact with others and join in the conversation once you have an idea of how they work.
3. Spend ten minutes a day updating your social media. Share things about what you are doing and one post about your books as well as sharing and commenting on others posts.

16

KEYWORDS AND CATEGORIES

Keywords

KEYWORDS ARE USED online to increase your book's visibility and allow it to rank higher in the search engines of online shops. For most writers this will mean Amazon. A quick search of the internet will give you thousands of articles on this topic. They all agree it is worth spending time to get your keywords right. This is one of the main ways in which readers can discover your books. The beauty of this is that it can be done from your computer sitting at home.

WHEN YOU ARE DECIDING on keywords, you should be thinking like a customer. What would a customer search for if they are looking for a particular genre of book? As a note, keywords cannot include your title, or subjective claims about quality such as bestselling. Amazon has been clamping down on these recently and has been removing them. You can't add something like new either as this is only a temporary. Amazon recommends that you use the following guide:

Setting
Themes
Character roles
Character types
Story tone

So taking these individually you could use:

Setting - Scottish, English, British, International, Contemporary Scotland, Jacobean Scotland
Okay I'm Scottish so bear with me here.

Themes - revenge, psychological, coming of age

Character roles - strong female lead, bullied teenager,

Character types - single mother, single father, transgender teen, harried detective

Story tone - gritty, realistic, dystopian

THESE ARE JUST examples from both Amazon and myself. I am sure as writers you will be able to think of many more. You can also find keywords on Amazon by typing in the beginning of a word and up will come some suggested keywords. This may be laborious but it does work.

A COMBINATION of these can be used to make long tailed keywords. Amazon will allow you to use phrases. So for my crime books I could use:

GRITTY SCOTTISH CRIME
   Gritty Crime Contemporary Scotland
   Tartan Noir - This is a style of Scottish Crime Writing and people will actually search using this term. It is worth exploring if there are any such titles that fit your genre or country

IF YOU ARE TRADITIONALLY PUBLISHED, then your publisher will set the key words. If you are an indie author, you can change the keywords as often as you want. If your books are selling well, then leave the keywords be. If you would like to boost sales, then it is worth exploring different keywords.

I WILL SAY one more thing about keywords. Amazon only allows for a certain number of words/characters in this section when you set the book up. However, they come into their own when considering ads. More about this later. Some authors try to get round this by stuffing as many keywords as possible in brackets after the main title. I would advise you not to do this for a number of reasons. It looks both unprofessional and, I think, a little desperate. You will have spent time choosing your title and ensuring it shows your book in its best light. Why ruin it by including a lot of random words at the end. It is also against Amazon's terms and conditions.

An example of this stuffing could be:

Kill Now (edge of your seat, gripping Scottish crime thriller with a twist that you won't see coming)

Despite it being against Amazon's terms and conditions you will still see some of these getting through. Whether you do it or not is up to you. Only you can make the call but my advice would be – don't do it.

This is one area it is worth taking time over. Ask other authors what keywords they use. Do searches for different keywords and see what comes up on Google, Bing, or any other search engine. If it is Amazon which comes up first, then it is probably a keyword which Amazon uses. This can be one of the best ways to get your books noticed, so not something to take lightly.

There are programmes which can help you find both key words and categories, and these can save a lot of time and effort, not only for your book metadata but also when doing Amazon ads. I appreciate I covered Amazon ads in a previous chapter but I want to explain about the keywords you use. For each ad, and you will need to run many of them to find ones which work; you will need 100-150 unique keywords. This may seem like an impossible task, but there are two programmes which make these easy.

. . .

Publisher Rocket

THIS IS an app you download to your computer. It does cost money but, let me tell you, it is worth every penny. It makes short work of finding both keywords and categories for your books. I will come back to categories in a moment. This programme covers four areas:

1. Keyword Search
2. Competition Analyser
3. Category Search
4. AMS Keyword Search (AMS = Amazon Marketing Services)

Keywords are what you use in your books' metadata and ads. Competition Analyser and Category Search are to do with categories.

Categories

CATEGORIES ARE what you put your book into on Amazon, Apple Books, Kobo ,and Ingram Spark. These determine who is shown your book when they type a keyword into the search bar when they are looking for a book. You choose the categories when you set your book up. So, taking Amazon as an example. My *DI Shona McKenzie* Books are in the following categories:

1. Scottish crime
2. Serial killers

3. British detectives

That is what shows up on Amazon but they are actually in ten categories. You can email Amazon and tell them what specific categories you would like them to appear under.

Using Publisher Rocket you can use both competition analyser and categories to decide the ten best categories for your book. Many authors use this to make sure they are in the best categories to hit number one on Amazon.

BKLNK

Is a free book category and marketing tool which is web based. This also gives Universal Book Links. So a useful tool to have handy.

I use both together to make sure I do the best for my books. This is an area worth taking the time to get right as it can make a significant difference in terms of discoverability and ultimately sales.

EXERCISE

1. Brainstorm some keywords for your books.
2. If you would like more traction on Amazon, check your keywords. Do they adequately convey the tone and genre of your book?

3. If you are an indie author, change your keywords for one book on Amazon.

4. If you are not yet published, start to think about what keywords would suit books in your genre. Keep these in a notebook specifically for your book. Add to them as more come to mind.

5. Take time to explore BKLNK and get to grips with ways in which it can help you with your metadata.

17

AUTHOR PAGES

Your author page, whatever platform may hold it, is your window to the outside world. It is the space for you to showcase yourself and your books. This means it is worthwhile spending time, energy, and resources on this aspect of your marketing. It is also one of the easiest parts of your marketing strategy to get right.

MAKE this the best page it can be. Spend money on a professional photo. This is not the time for that photo taken on a day trip to Blackpool. This is the opportunity for you to show yourself as a professional and someone who pays attention to detail. Your author bio should also reflect you as both a person and a professional. I had a professional photo shoot done in London at Hatton Garden. The photographer has also done shoots with several of the tops models. This was a significant investment as it was not cheap and involved a trip to London as I live in Scotland. However, I was blown away by the results, and I was able to take a friend and have photos done with her as well, so I considered it worth it.

WHEN CONSIDERING your Amazon Author Page, all published books should be there, with covers, and blurbs, which catch the reader's attention. Your branding will show here in glorious technicolour detail. This is one of the reasons why it is worth investing in branding your covers over all the books in a series. This needs to be updated the minute a new book is available. A couple of things to note:

1. The author page for each country must be done individually. You cannot update the USA and then have it appear everywhere.

2. Not all countries have the ability for an Amazon Author Page. At the time of writing the following countries have this functionality:

USA
UK
Japan
Germany
France

I have no clue why this is the case but it must make business sense to Amazon. As a side note – you are not able to set up pre-orders in India. No, I don't know why that is the case either.

YOU SET up your Author Page from Amazon Author Central for each country.

. . .

MAKE sure the author page on your website is up to date and contains all the books which you have written. It is so easy to forget this part of the website when in the throes of launching a book. I am saying this from experience. I often remember weeks after it comes out, to add a book to my website. If you are an indie author you will be able to change your Amazon Author Page as well by going to Amazon Author Central.

EXERCISE

1. Check your Amazon Author page. Is it showing you in the best light?
2. Make any required changes.
3. Do the same for your website author page.
4. If you are available for talks, workshops, or book signings add this to you website author page.

18

PODCASTING

As a writer, there are a number of ways in which podcasts can help you market your book. These are:

1. Listening to podcasts on book marketing by industry experts.
2. Appearing as a guest on established podcasts.
3. Podcasters talking about you and your books.
4. Hosting your own podcast.

Podcasts lead to increased discoverability and can also lead to increased speaking engagements, so it is worth exploring guesting on them or hosting your own.,

LISTENING to Podcasts

THERE ARE a number of excellent podcasts on writing and marketing available. The ones I have found to be most useful and highly recommend are:

The Creative Penn
http://www.thecreativepenn.com/podcasts/

The Sell More Books Show http://sellmorebooksshow.com

The Creative Writers Toolbelt http://ajc-cwt-001.podomatic.com

The Alliance of Independent Authors https://itunes.apple.com/us/podcast/alli-author-advice-centre/id1080135033?mt=2

The writing and Marketing Show (hosted by one Wendy H. Jones) https://www.wendyhjones.com/writing-and-marketing/podcasts/

Go Publish Yourself https://podcasts.apple.com/gb/podcast/go-publish-yourself-an-ingramspark-podcast/id1328544675

THESE ARE all podcasts which have been running for some time. They are also by industry experts who have a lot of experience in the field of writing and marketing. You can subscribe to each of these on iTunes or from the relevant websites.

I LISTEN to podcasts when I am in the car or when exercising. Not only does this pass the time but allows me to learn at the same time. I have gained a lot of valuable insight from these podcasts. I have been listening to *The Creative Penn* since the beginning of my author journey and it has helped to shape that journey.

THERE ARE ALSO PODCASTERS who interview writers in different genres. It is worth exploring these to find out what podcasts are available in your genre. I am subscribed to one called *Crime Writers On* ... You may also find podcasts for your local area. Whatever you come up with I am sure there is a podcast out there for it.

GUESTING on a Podcast

ALL OF THESE podcasts have featured guests. This is a chance to hear from an industry expert in a particular niche. I have guested on several podcasts including *The Creative Writers Toolbelt,* run by Andrew Chamberlain. This is an excellent podcast which talks mainly about writing. Andrew is a creative writing tutor and his advice is sound and helpful. It was a thrill to be invited along. Andrew sent me the questions in advance. The recording was simply done through Skype. I moved into the dining room with my laptop for the recording. This is because my office used to be a garage so echoes a little. The sound was clearer in the carpeted and well insulated dining room. This is something to think about if you are invited to be a guest.

IT IS important to prepare for the interview and to jot down notes on what you might say. Don't stick rigidly to this though, or you may come across as wooden. It can be a lot of fun, so relax and enjoy yourself. It is also useful to know a bit about the person who has invited you and the podcast on which you will be guesting.

AFTER THE PODCAST IS FINISHED, you may be sent a raw copy to listen to before it goes out. This is your chance to ask for something to be taken out if you do not like the sound of it. Obviously, only use this if you have to, otherwise the podcast may sound strange.

THE BEAUTY of this is that not only is your podcast on iTunes, but you can share it elsewhere. I have uploaded it to my own website, and it is also on a number of other websites. This spreads the word far and wide and the reach rises exponentially with every share.

SOCIAL SHARING through Podcasts

ALTHOUGH YOU MAY NOT BE INVITED to guest on a podcast, the podcasters may sometimes talk about you and your books. On the *Sell More Book Show* podcast you have an opportunity to support the show on Patreon. If you do this, then they will mention your book on the show. You may also find that podcasters talk about books by other authors if they like the books. You obviously cannot manufacture this, but if it happens, it is more valuable than a priceless jewel.

SETTING up Your Own Podcast

. . .

THIS IS SLIGHTLY MORE complex than the other methods as it involves time, expens,e and some level of expertise. However, these steps can be learned and it is worth the investment to do so. But why? Why would you want to do a podcast in the first place? There are a number of reasons:

1. You have an idea for a subject.
2. It's a way of helping others.
3. You can build your brand name.
4. It is fun.

IN ORDER TO start a podcast you will need:

1. A good quality microphone. This is important because sound quality is important to ensure the end product is of a high quality.
2. A quiet space in which to record. I use my sitting room with the curtains closed on both windows. I do this to deaden the sound and to stop it bouncing off the glass in the windows. My office used to be a garage so there is too much of an echo due to the brick walls.
3. A recording device such as a PC or Mac.
4. Recording software. Audacity.com is very highly regarded ,but I use Garageband as I have a Mac. I did look into using Audacity but after a telephone discussion with both Audacity and Apple, I discovered that Audacity did not work with the latest OSX. You will have to take time to get used to all the functions. YouTube was my friend as I worked out all the intricacies of the software. However, after several weeks I am now more confident.
5. Podcast host to store your podcast. These include

Buzzsprout (which I use), Podomatic, Libsyn, and Podbean. These will give you an RSS feed to use in the places that listeners will find you. The most famous one of these is Apple Podcasts, but there are numerous others such as Spotify, Stitcher, Google Podcast, and iHeart Radio amongst others. You can also put it on your own website. One exciting thing for me was when I said, "Alexa, play the *Writing and Marketing Show* on TuneIn." Then my voice came out of my Amazon Echo. Okay, I'm easily pleased but it is another way that listeners can find you in another way.

6. If you want a jingle, then you must make sure you do not fall foul of copyright. There are various companies you can get free music from but this usually means that you have to tell the listener where the music came from every time you use it. I paid for the jingle from a company called Purple Planet Music, and this means I can use it for anything at any time with no attribution.

THINK CAREFULLY about how you will start and end your podcast. This should be the same in every podcast. You may want to have a jingle as well. This will identify your podcast to your listeners. To get an idea of ways in which to start and end your podcasts, listen to some. You may want to start with the podcasts I have outlined above. I recorded my intro and outro and I then stitch them into the show each week. This is quick and easy to do.

AUDACITY AND GARAGEBAND will not only allow you to record your interview, but allows you to clip out the bits that you don't want such as silences or uhms and ahs. It is important to ensure that your podcast is professionally produced and sounds good.

I KNOW there are people who do not like Podcasts and you may be one of them. I appreciate where you are coming from. We all like different things. I would ask you to think back to what I said at the beginning of the book. It is what the reader enjoys that is important. You need to meet your readers at the place they are at. If you ignore podcasts in their entirety, you are ignoring those who listen to podcasts and will hear about your books in that way. You may not want to set up your own Podcast but think about being a guest on one.

EXERCISE

1. Choose one of the recommended podcasts and listen to some of the episodes .
2. Do a search for Podcasts which might interest you. Listen to one episode of a few of them.
3. Contact one person who runs a Podcast and ask them if they are looking for guests.

19

PUBLIC SPEAKING

Speaking engagements are a way of meeting new readers, getting your name out there, and selling books. Again, they can also be a lot of fun. How do we find these speaking engagements? I have done this in a number of ways. Obviously, these have worked for me, but you may have to think of your own methods. You can use my ideas as a springboard for the public speaking part of your Power Packed Marketing Plan.

CONTACT your local librarians and explain that you are a local author. Ask them if they would like you to do a talk. They may say that you will have to contact the head librarian for the region. Others have the authority to book you in themselves. Be ready to explain what your book is about and why it would fit in with that particular library. For example, the main detective in my book, DI Shona McKenzie, lives in Broughty Ferry. Therefore, Broughty Ferry library were keen for me to do a talk. My books are popular in Dundee libraries, so I have managed to do an Author Talk in most of these.

ONE IMPORTANT THING TO REMEMBER, if you give a number of talks in a small geographical area, you must ensure that you vary your topics. Whilst on the whole, the audience will be different, there may be some who come to everything. To be honest, I have found that this makes sure that I keep the talks fresh and lively. This will come across to anyone who is in the audience and you will sound more natural. If you are bored with your talks, this comes across when you present them and the readers who have come to hear you will pick up on that.

LOCAL GROUPS ARE OFTEN LOOKING for speakers. These include Rotary Clubs, women's groups, educational groups, writers groups, and the Women's Institute among many others. I have found that when I'm doing book signings I have been approached by people looking for speakers for their groups. The library and bookshops have also advised people to contact me when they're looking for speakers. When local organisations start to recognise that you are a competent and confident speaker, they recommend you to others. Being funny also helps. You are free to contact as many groups as you think is appropriate.

THERE IS much discussion and debate at the moment regarding payment for public speaking and events. I agree that authors should be paid for their time in preparing for the event and the event itself. However, I made the decision that I will talk at libraries and schools for free. My reasoning behind this is that very often these institutions have very little budget for visiting speakers. I do, however, ask if I'm allowed to sell books. The answer has always been yes and I have always sold enough books to make it worth my while attending the events. You will need to make the decision as to what is acceptable for you. There is one exception to this rule. If the event is funded by the Scottish Book Trust, there will be payment for the speaker. The library, or school, will then be expected to pay you, and I do expect payment under those circumstances.

When I do talks for public groups, I do expect payment. This has never been a problem and all groups have been willing to pay. I also sell books at these events.

ONE THING TO CONSIDER, although you can sell books at author events, it is not guaranteed that you will sell many or even any. I use them as a promotional tool as well as an opportunity to sell books. Take postcards and business cards along and hand these out to participants. You may sell books down the line either through bookshops, your website, or online stores.

Another way, which you can support others whilst getting your name known, and selling books, are writers' workshops or courses. I have been asked to run individual workshops and a short beginner's course. It is worth looking out for opportunities such as these. Not only will you be helping local communities, but it is also a chance for you to sell books. Again, the focus is not on selling your books but in supporting others to move their own writing forward.

. . .

SINCE MY FIRST book came out, I have developed my public speaking internationally. I have spoken at conferences and events in countries around the world including, Southern Ireland, the USA, and Canada. I have also spoken at numerous conferences in the UKand have done book tours throughout the UK and USA. Look for those opportunities and apply to speak. Once you are accepted, make sure you give a powerful talk. Once your name becomes known as delivering quality talks, you will start to be invited rather than applying. I have spoken at some conferences more than once.

WHEN YOU ARE at these events, networking is key. I have made several good friends from around the world and this has also led to more speaking engagements. I reiterate what I said previously – be nice to people and invariably they are nice back. Also, you never know where it might lead.

EXERCISE

1. Identify groups in your local area who may be looking for speakers.
2. Approach one of these groups and ask them if they would be interested in you doing a talk.
3. Approach your local library and discuss the possibility of your doing an author talk.

20

SHORT TAIL VERSUS LONG TAIL PROMOTION

In a nutshell, short tailed marketing is reducing the price of an item and seeing a spike in sales. It is also releasing a new book and seeing a spike in sales. Long tailed marketing is reducing the price of one item in order to sell the more lucrative items in your store. Supermarkets employ this extremely successfully with their loss leaders.

FOR AUTHORS, this may mean selling the first book in the series at a reduced price in order to sell the other books in the series at full price. It could also mean reducing the price of the book briefly for a paid promotion in the expectation that the book will continue to sell after the promotion is finished. This may happen because the paid promotion drives the book up the charts. It is then in a good position to be noticed by potential readers. Short tailed promotion will hopefully give you a spike in sales on the day of the promotion. However, as an author the long tail effect is most important for long-term success. This will provide steady income throughout the life of your books. This involves long-term promotion of your books.

THERE IS a strong argument that having one book in a series perma-free can boost sales of the remaining books in the series. If you have several books under your belt, this may be something that you would like to try. I have not yet tried this; however, I am told that many authors have used it successfully. If you feel that you do not have enough books out as yet to go for a perma-free book, reducing the price of the first in series can also work. You will need to work out the price point to which you are willing to lower your book. There is a strong argument for this price point to be £0.99 or $0.99. I have read recently that £1.99/$1.99 is not a good price point for an ebook at the time of writing this. However, I cannot say if this is the case. It may be worth trying out different price points to see which works for you.

ONE POINT OF NOTE, this may only be possible if you are an indie author. Those who are traditionally published may not have the flexibility to adjust prices. It may also be worth looking at having different books on promotion at different times. Bryan Cohen in his successful *Sell More Books Show* podcast puts forward the thought that as one book comes off promotion put the next one on. This can cause a ripple effect which can lead to long term book sales.

21

WHERE IN THE WORLD

Unless you are living at the bottom of the ocean you will probably have noticed there are numerous versions of books - hardback, paperback, ebook and audiobook. You can buy books from many different places. Traditionally, books were purchased from chain and independent bookshops. For several years now you have been able to download books straight to ereaders from stores such as Amazon, Kobo, iBooks, Nook, Google Play, and Smashwords. You can also get them from subscription services such as Scribd. In my previous book, I talked about Oyster but they have since closed their doors. I tell you this to say that it is worth following the industry news carefully. Libraries are packed with books in all formats and these can be borrowed for free. Supermarkets stock books and airports have vending machines for books. Readers can also buy books from author and publisher websites. In fact they are everywhere. "Why is she telling me this I hear you ask? I already know that."

. . .

THIS LIST of places to buy books is important for one very good reason. If you want to sell books, you should be in as many places as possible. Okay, the airport vending machine version might be a bit trickier and I think you have to offer sacrifices at dawn to get into airport bookshops, but the rest are up for grabs.

FIRSTLY, make sure that your books are out in all formats. Whilst many readers are now turning to ebooks, there are still an equal number who will read physical books. Audio books are becoming increasingly more popular. At the end of 2019, it was reported that 1 in 5 American's listen to audio books on a regular basis. Many readers bounce between both. I know I certainly do. People now lead busy lives and find themselves driving long distances. Surveys have shown that readers will listen to audiobooks to pass the time.

AT THE TIME of writing this book, I am currently in the process of working with a narrator to get my first *DI Shona McKenzie* book, *Killer's Countdown*, narrated for audiobook. If you have a traditional publisher, they will deal with the audiobook production. If you are an Indie author, then you will need to deal with Amazon ACX to get your book narrated and published as an audiobook. The process for this could be a whole book in itself. I will not be discussing this in here and would advise you to research it carefully before going ahead. I will say one last thing about audio books. There are two ways in which you can work with a narrator. The first is to pay them up front. This way all profits from the book will belong to you. If you wish to go down this route, then you will need to make sure you have the upfront cost which can run to thousands of pounds. The other way is to profit share through ACX. This way Amazon/Audible will pay the narrator and the author half of the profits of the audiobook. This will be for the lifetime of the book. However, once you go down the profit share route, you will be contracted to Amazon for that book for seven years. This is something about which you should think carefully.

If you do want to explore audio, I would recommend *Audio For Authors: Audiobooks, Podcasting, And Voice Technologies* by Joanna Penn. I have this book and it gives cutting edge advice which will take you through the process. Once your book is available in all formats, then my advice would be to go for as wide a distribution as possible. If you are an indie author, you will have total control over this.

SOME AUTHORS ARGUE that it is better to stay exclusive to Amazon through a programme called KDP Select. This means that your book will be available for readers to borrow to read through Kindle Unlimited and you are paid per page read as I outlined previously. It also means Amazon will advertise and promote your book more freely. You will receive larger royalties per book in all markets. However, my advice would be to go wide and have your book available everywhere. This allows you to grow a readership on other platforms and reach a wider audience. You will obviously need to decide which method will work for you. It may be that you would like to try one of your books in KDP Select for a period of 90-days. This is the minimum length of time you can have your book in the programme. During this time you can reduce the price, or even make the book free, on selected days. Amazon is also likely to promote your book.

At the end of 90-days you can pull your book from KDP Select and publish on other platforms, although this means you are starting from scratch on all platforms, including, surprisingly, Amazon.

ANOTHER ASPECT of marketing concerns the title of this chapter - 'Where in the World?' The answer to that should be everywhere it is possible to be. Ebooks are available in most countries in the world so that is not an issue. Pricing, however, is an issue. Different countries will sustain different pricing points. Books can be more expensive in Australia and Canada as readers are used to this. However, if you wish to sell books in India, you will need to price your books at 77 India Rupees. This is because readers in India are accustomed to buying books more cheaply. I am also reliably informed that in India prices ending in 7 are the sweet spot, just as prices ending in 9 are the sweet spot in UK/USA. At the time of writing, ebooks are becoming more popular in India due, for the most part, to the rise in mobile phone use. I would advise you to think carefully about the price of your book in different markets. It is worth doing some research in this area.

DISTRIBUTING paperback books worldwide is slightly different. If your books are available in paperback on Amazon, they will be available for purchase in:

UK
USA
Canada
France

Germany
Spain
India
Brazil
Mexico
Japan
Australia
All via the Amazon store.

I WOULD STRONGLY ADVISE you to use Amazon for Amazon paperback sales only and turn off extended distribution. This means distribution to stores and libraries. For extended distribution use Ingram Spark. Ingram has a wider reach and bookshops are also more likely to order books via Ingram than Amazon. This makes sound business sense. I can walk into any bookshop in the world, ask for a copy of my book, and it will be ordered for me. I know this because I have tested it. I have even seen my books on the shelves of bookshops in the USA. Now that's a thrill, let me tell you.

THERE IS ALSO a ripple effect from having books both locally and internationally. You may start off by selling books locally, particularly if your books are set in your local area. If those readers like the books, they will tell their friends about it and this moves nationally. They then have friends living abroad and they tell them. They tell their friends and so an international readership is born. We are now living globally and there will be a global response to your books. In fact, everyone expects to be able to buy your books everywhere. I have had requests from Lesotho as to where my books can be bought. At the time of writing, I have sold books in UK, USA, Spain, France, Germany, Netherlands, Canada, New Zealand, Australia, Mexico, Hong Kong, Japan, Poland, and India. I am working on being sold in every country in the world.

WHATEVER YOU DO, do not miss, or turn down, an opportunity to get your book in front of readers. Seize all of the above opportunities and use them in a way which will work for you. You do not need to do all of this all at once, but wait for the right opportunity. *Killer's Countdown* has been out for 4 years and I am only now considering an audiobook.

EXERCISE

1. Do an audit of where your book is available for both vendors and geographically.
2. If you are lacking in any area, consider if this is somewhere you would like your book to be.
3. Write an action plan to ensure your book is available in all locations.

22

WHAT NOW

I am sure by now your head is spinning with all the things you feel you have to do to sell your books. You may be feeling overwhelmed and thinking, this is not for me. It is important to remember that even doing a few of these steps will help you to sell more books. I cannot promise you that you will be a multimillion selling author, but I can promise you that it will get you and your books noticed. Getting noticed in the right way will bring sales.

THE OLD SAYING, every journey starts with a single step is equally true for marketing. This step for you is to choose one thing you feel you could do from this book. Focus on that and start to do it today. Brainstorm ways that it could work for you.

ONE THING that I did was buy a yearly planner for my wall. I then plot down on there what I am doing for marketing for each week of the year. Some weeks I may have several things on the plan. Other weeks I may only have one. However, I can see at a glance where I am going with my marketing. Do this and write down just one marketing activity per week. That means you have 52 new opportunities to market your book. This is going to help you in more ways than you can ever imagine. As your book sales grow, put money aside to be used for marketing. As you continue to market and promote your book, your sales will grow. This is not a race but a marathon. Keep going and you will see the results.

WRITING and publishing more books should be a large part of your marketing plan. In fact, it should be the largest part. The number one way to market your books is to write more books. Very often, before buying a book, readers will look to see how many other books the author has written. I do that all the time as I like to know there are more if I invest in that author. If a reader enjoys an author's book, they will often go and buy several others immediately after finishing it. Books sell books. Hence the reason I am currently investing my paid advertising in the first book in all my series. This makes sound business sense as I am looking for read through rate. This means the number of books a reader buys after they have read the first one in the series. My read through rate is high, so readers are invested in the series. I am not saying everyone who picks up my first book will carry on through all six, but many do.

THIS LEADS me on to the back matter in your book. This should have the names of all the other books you have written. In the case of digital books, it should also have links to buy these books. You may also want to include the first chapter of your next book. This is also an incentive to make sure that the opening chapters of your next book are dynamic and attention grabbing. Make them end on a cliff-hanger so readers want to know what happens next. I will add one thing here, some readers really do not like the fact that there is so called, bonus material, at the end of a book. They feel short changed as they were expecting the book to continue for several more pages and suddenly the book is at an end and the rest is a different book. Also, remember, when you pay for copies of your book, the price per copy depends on page count. This is another area where you will need to make a business decision. Is it worth the extra cost for the book to advertise the next in series?

THE MOST IMPORTANT thing to remember about marketing is that you should have fun. If you are dreading everything you do in terms of marketing, then it is time to rethink your marketing strategy. Yes, you may need to step outside your comfort zone. That is inevitable. However, you should not be miserable in the process. Use this book to guide you and to give you inspiration. Decide which of these methods you will use, if any. Use it to give form to your own ideas and develop your own unique, individualised marketing plan.

BY NOW YOU SHOULD HAVE, at the very least, a basic marketing plan in place. You may now have a detailed plan and be keen and ready to get cracking. Whatever stage you are at, I would encourage you to take steps to market your book starting right now. I wish you all the very best with your books and your sales.

23

RECOMMENDED RESOURCES

There are a number of excellent resources to help you to develop your marketing plan. These are some which I found highly valuable. Please note these are under categories and in alphabetical order. The order they are in does not indicate any one of these being any better than the others. These are all excellent resources in their own right. They are not all overtly, marketing books, but I believe they all have value within the marketing process.

BOOKS

CABALLO, Frances, (2012), *Social Media Just for Writers: The Best Online Marketing Tips for Selling Your Books*, Act Communications

As the name suggests this is a book on social media for writing. It is jam packed full of useful information and recommended resources and links.

Carvill, Michelle and Taylor, David, (2013), *The Business of Being Social*, Crimson Publishing Ltd.
This book takes you through the process of using social media marketing in a small business setting.

Conlon, Ciara, (2016), *Productivity for Dummies*, John Wiley and Sons
As writers, one of the main objections to marketing is that we do not have time. This book will help you to look at how you manage your time and work towards using it more effectively.

Cohen, Bryan, (2016), *How to Write a Sizzling Synposis*, Bryan Cohen
How to write blurbs and ad copy.

Corder, Honoree, (2015), *Propserity for Writers: A Writer's Guide to Creating Abundance*, Honoree Enterprises Publishing
This takes a different approach in that it helps you to change your mindset about marketing.

Jones, Wendy H. (2019), *Motivation Matters*, Scott and Lawson
366 Exercises to help you change your mindset about writing and get you writing every day.

Lancaster, Paul and Shenck Barabara, (2014), *Small Business Marketing for Dummies*, John Wiley and Sons
Chock full of good advice about the basics of marketing.

Penn, Joanna, (2015), *How to make a Living with your Writing*, Curl Up Press
Jam packed full of advice on how to make a living from writing your books.

Young, Debbie, (2015), *Sell Your Books: A Book Promotion Handbook for the Self-Published or Indie Author*, Silverwood Books
Takes you through the process of book marketing.

. . .

WEBSITES

1. The Creative Penn (https://www.
   thecreativepenn.com)
2. Wendy H. Jones Author (https://www.
   wendyhjones.com/writing-and-marketing/)
3. The Sell More Books Show
   (https://sellmorebooksshow.com)
4. Jessica Bell (https://www.jessicabellauthor.com)

ABOUT THE AUTHOR

Wendy H. Jones is the author of the International Best Selling, Award Winning crime series *The DI Shona McKenzie Mysteries*, *The Cass Claymore Investigates* Series, *The Fergus and Flora Mysteries*, and the *Bertie the Buffalo* series of children's picture books. After a career in the military, she moved into Academia, where she wrote for academic publications and textbooks. She has had extensive marketing training throughout her career. After a period of illness, she moved back to her native Scotland where she settled in Dundee and started to write novels. She loves writing but has embraced the marketing aspect of the role with enthusiasm. On meeting people, they often greet her with, "I saw you at …. You're everywhere." This is possibly quite true, as she loves meeting readers and talking about both books and writing. She is also a skilled public speaker, having presented on writing at a number of International Conferences, and has developed this to include presentations on marketing your books.

ALSO BY WENDY H. JONES

Writing Matters Series

Motivation Matters

DI Shona McKenzie Mysteries

Killer's Countdown

Killer's Craft

Killer's Cross

Killer's Cut

Killer's Crew

Killer's Crypt

Cass Claymore Investigates

Antiques and Alibis

Bertie the Buffalo Series

Bertie the Buffalo

Bertie the Buffalo Colouring Book

Women's Motivational

The Power of Why

Women Win Against All Odds

Christian Living

New Life: Reflections for Lent

Merry Christmas Everyone